French - Polish

LEARNING FLASHCARDS

FOR BABIES TODDLERS

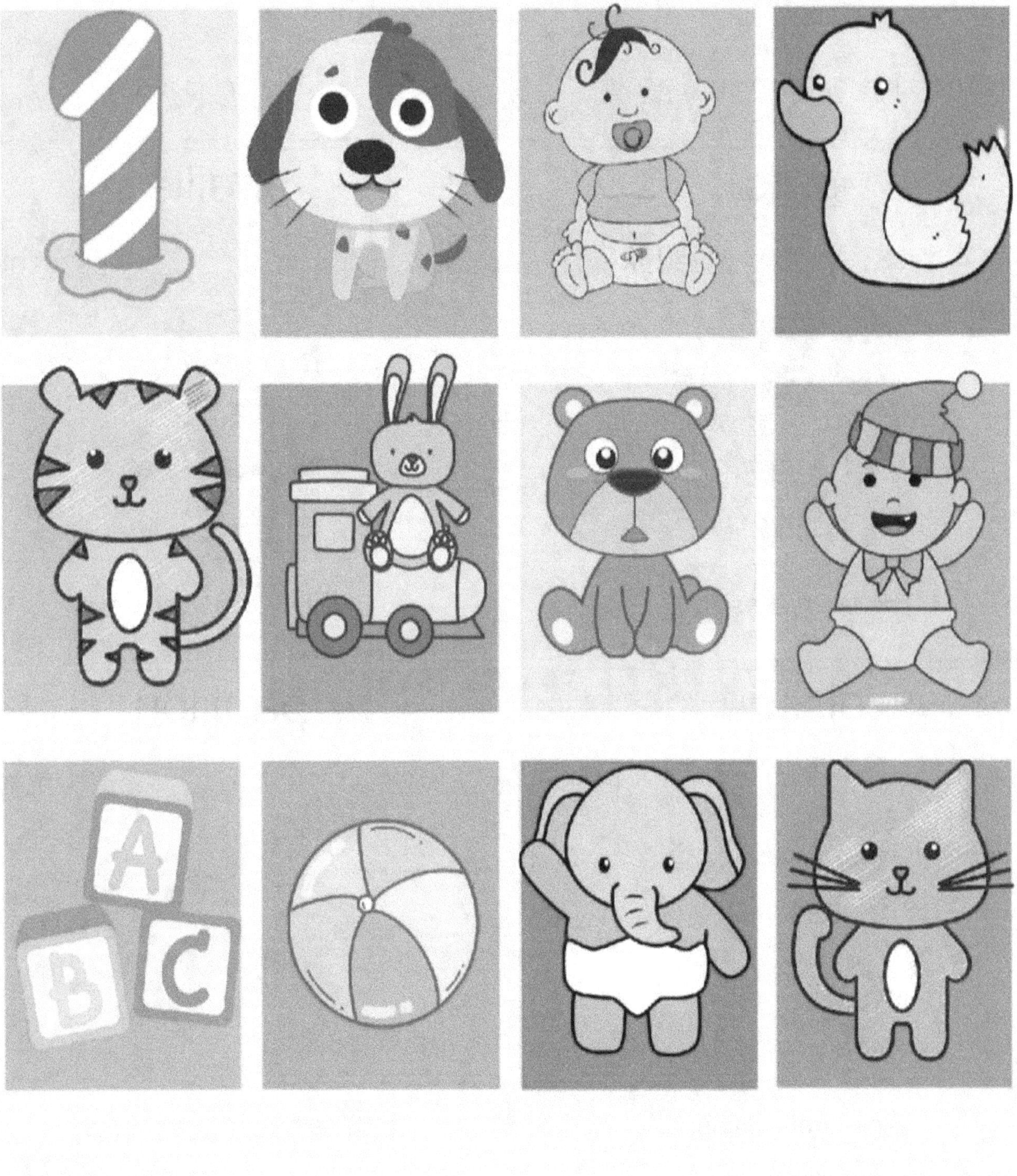

alligator

aligator

The alligator is having a party.

fourmi

mrówka

The ant is red.

ours

niedźwiedź

The bear loves you.

abeille

pszczoła

The bee is saying hello.

oiseau

ptak

The bird is flying.

papillon

motyl

The butterfly is pretty.

chameau

wielbłąd

The camel has a hump.

chat

kot

The cat is happy.

dinosaure

dinozaur

The dinosaur is laying eggs.

poulet

kurczak

The chicken is dancing.

vache

krowa

The cow has a bell.

cerf

jeleń

The reindeer has a toy.

chien

pies

The dog has two floppy ears.

dauphin

delfin

The dolphin is swimming.

canard

kaczka

The duck has a bow.

aigle

orzeł

The eagle is looking for food.

l'éléphant

słoń

The elephant is sitting.

poisson

ryba

The fish is a clownfish.

libellule

ważka

The dragonfly is blue.

renard

lis

The fox has a red nose.

grenouille

żaba

The frog is smiling.

girafe

żyrafa

The giraffe has a long neck.

chèvre

koza

The goat has a beard

ver de terre

robak

The worm is in the apple

poule

kura

The hen has chicks.

hippopotame

hipopotam

The hippo is big.

cheval

koń

The horse is fast.

kangourou

kangur

The kangaroo has a baby.

chaton

kotek

The kitten is playing.

lion

lew

The lion has a mane.

homard

homar

The lobster is red.

singe

małpa

The monkey has a tail.

poulpe

ośmiornica

The octopus has food.

hibou

sowa

The owls have big eyes.

panda

panda

The panda wears a diaper.

porc

świnia

The pig is fat and pink.

chiot

szczeniak

The dog is brown.

lapin

królik

The rabbit has a carrot.

rat

szczur

The mouse is writing something.

crabe

krab

The crab has two pinchers.

requin

rekin

The shark is scary.

mouton

owca

The sheep are very fluffy.

escargot

ślimak

The snail is slow.

serpent

wąż

The snake has poison.

araignée

pająk

The spider is purple.

écureuil

wiewiórka

The squirrel has a nut.

tigre

tygrys

The tiger has a red bow.

tortue

żółw

The turtle has a shell.

loup

wilk

The wolf is smiling.

zèbre

zebra

The zebra is black and white.

dinde

indyk

The turkey has two legs.

coq

kogut

The rooster will crow.

perroquet

papuga

The parrot is colorful.

hérisson

jeż

The hedgehog has apples.

pomme

jabłko

The apple has a leaf.

abricot

morela

The apricot is yellow.

avocat

awokado

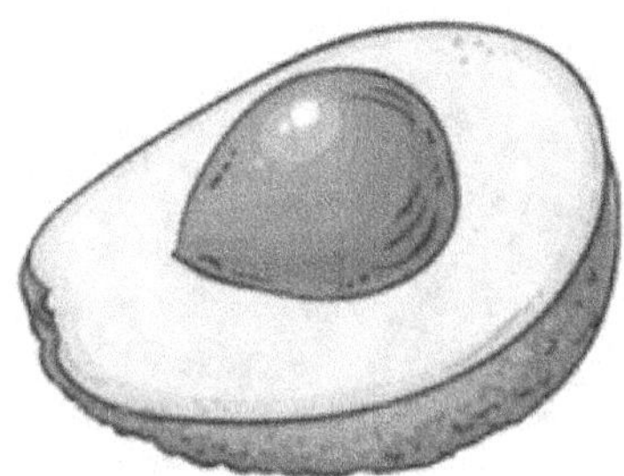

The avocado has a nut.

banane

banan

The banana is yellow.

la mûre

jeżyna

There are a lot of blackberries.

cassis

czarna porzeczka

The blackcurrants are yummy.

myrtille

borówka amerykańska

The blueberries are sweet.

cerise

wiśnia

The cherries have a stem.

noix de coco

orzech kokosowy

The coconuts have juice.

figues

figi

The fig has seeds.

grain de raisin

winogrono

The grapes are purple.

pamplemousse

grejpfrut

The grapefruits are sour.

kiwi

kiwi

The kiwi is fresh.

citron

cytrynowy

The lemons are yellow.

citron vert

limonka

We have lots of lime.

litchi

liczi

I like to eat lychee.

mandarine

mandarynka

Oranges are refreshing.

mangue

mango

Mango is my favorite fruit.

orange

pomarańczowy

Mandarins are like oranges.

papaye

papaja

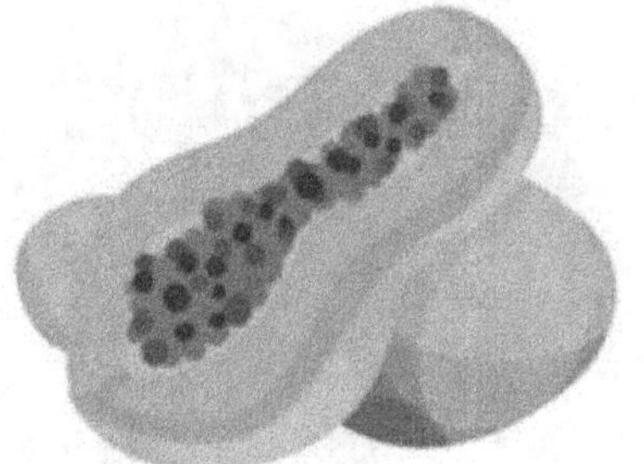

Papayas have lots of seeds.

pêche

brzoskwinia

Peaches are juicy.

poire

gruszka

Pears have a strange figure.

ananas

ananas

The pineapple has a thumbs up.

prune

śliwka

Plums are healthy for you.

grenade

granat

Pomegranates are all red.

framboise

malina

The raspberry is shiny.

fraise

truskawka

The strawberry has leaves on top.

pastèque

arbuz

The watermelon is big.

mandarine

mandarynka

The tangerine looks like an orange.

tarte

ciasto

I like to eat apple pie.

gâteau

ciasto

That cake is huge.

bonbons

cukierek

Candy is not good for your teeth.

biscuit

ciastko

Cookies are easy to make.

donut

pączek

I like strawberry donuts.

crème glacée

lody

The ice cream is melting.

muffin

muffinka

The muffin has a cute wrapper.

pudding

pudding

We eat pudding on Christmas.

classeur

spoiwo

I keep pictures in my binder.

livre

książka

I like to eat books.

sac à dos

plecak

The backpack has lots of stuff.

les ciseaux

nożyce

I have scissors in my bag.

épingles

szpilki

Pins can hold stuff up.

agrafe

spinacz

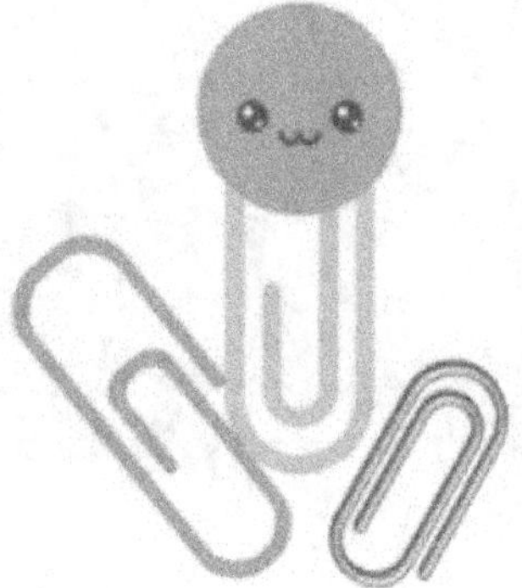

Clips can hold up paper.

papier

papier

I have lots of paper.

agrafeuse

zszywacz

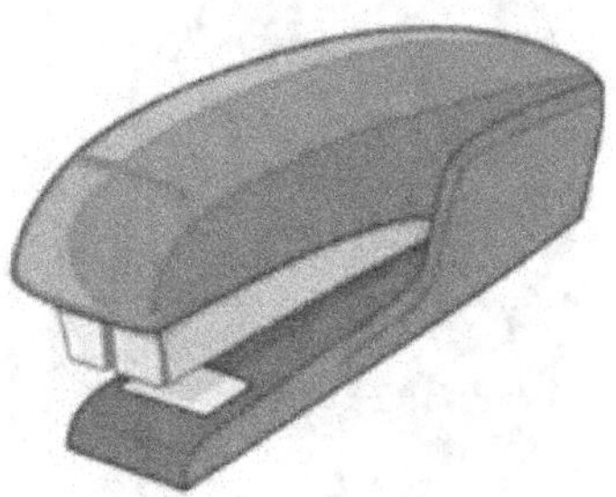

My stapler is shiny and red.

calculatrice

kalkulator

My calculator has buttons.

règle

linijka

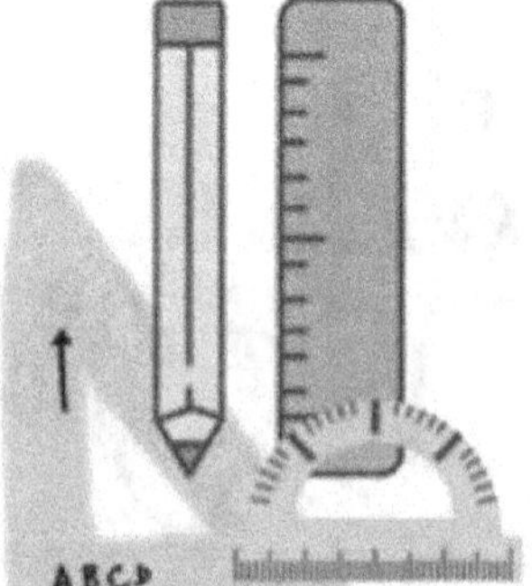

I have lots of rulers.

la colle

klej

The glue is sticky.

bibliothèque

półka na książki

My bookcase has lots of things.

calendrier

kalendarz

I have a calendar on my table.

chaise

krzesło

My chair is fancy.

l'horloge

zegar

The clock says that it's 3 o'clock.

ordinateur

komputer

I do things on my computer.

bureaux

biurka

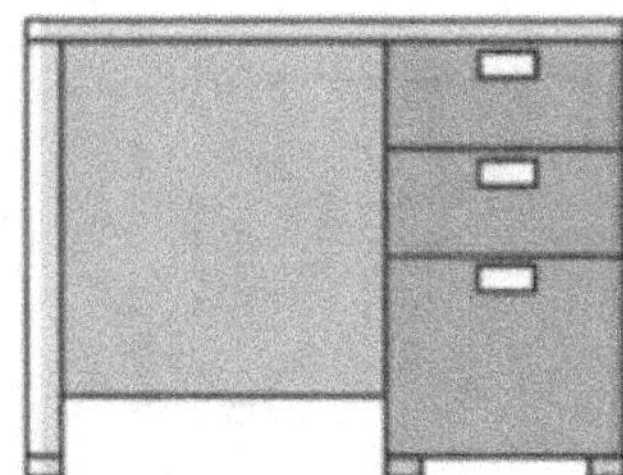

I put lots of things on my desk.

dictionnaire

słownik

The dictionary has lots of words.

la gomme

gumka do mazania

Erasers are used with pencils.

carte

mapa

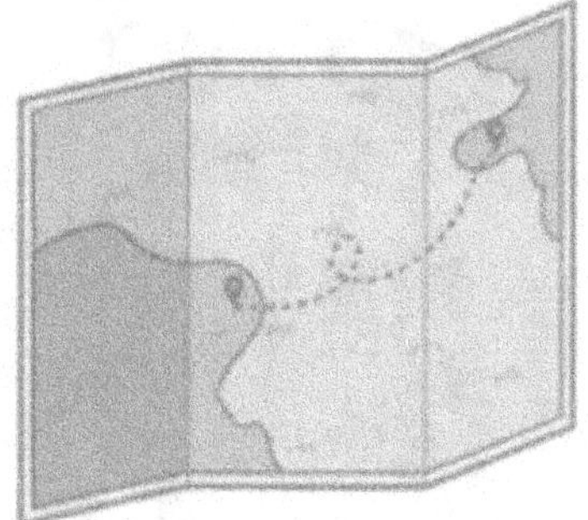

The map shows you different places.

carnet

notatnik

I use notebooks at school.

stylo

długopis

My pen is very pretty.

crayon

ołówek

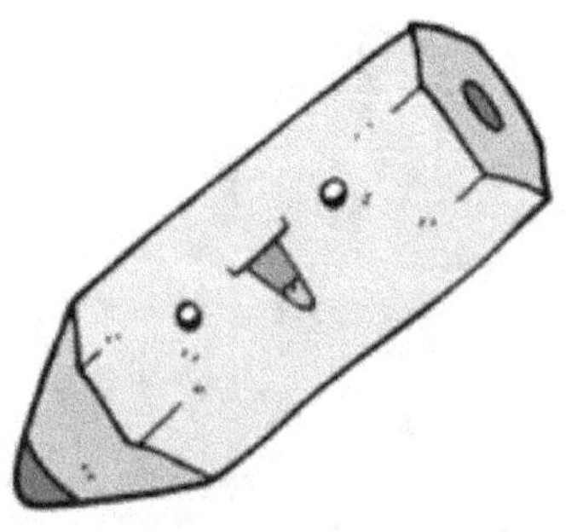

My friend gave me a pencil.

ceinture

pas

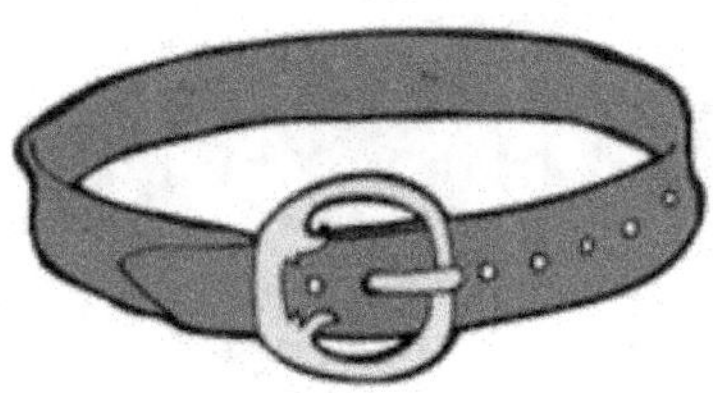

I have a belt on my pants.

bottes

buty

I have big brown boots.

chapeau

kapelusz

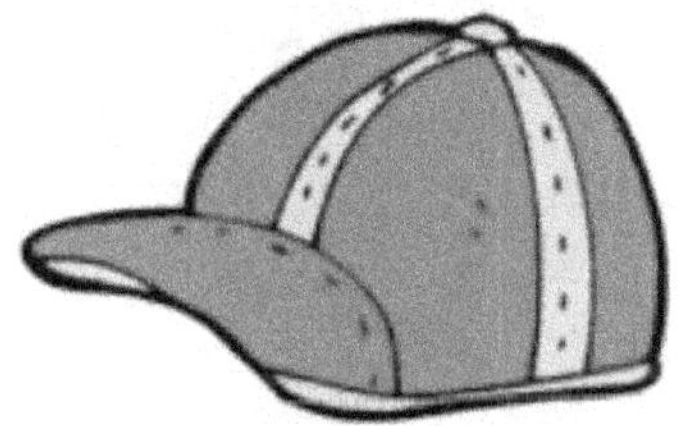

My mom bought me a new cap.

manteau

płaszcz

She has a long yellow coat.

robes

sukienki

My dress has a bow.

gants

rękawiczki

I got new gloves.

chapeau

kapelusz

That hat is for a wicked witch.

veste

kurtka

The jacket is cozy.

jeans

dżinsy

My jeans are long.

pyjamas

piżama

I sleep in my pajamas.

un pantalon

spodnie

The bear is wearing pants.

imperméable

płaszcz przeciwdeszczowy

We wear our raincoats when it is raining.

écharpe

szalik

The baby has a scarf around his neck.

chemise

koszula

I like this shirt the best.

des chaussures

buty

I have red and blue shoes.

jupe

spódnica

My skirt has lots of buttons.

pantalon

spodnie

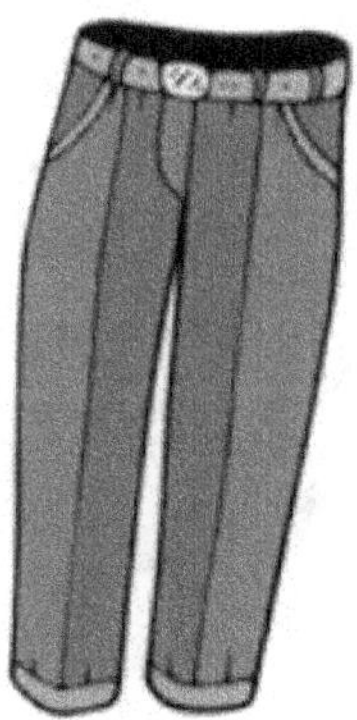

My dad wears slacks.

chaussons

kapcie

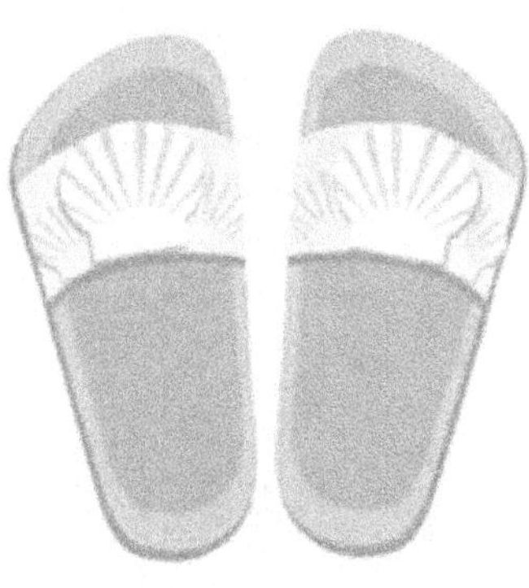

I have seashells on my sandals.

chaussettes

skarpety

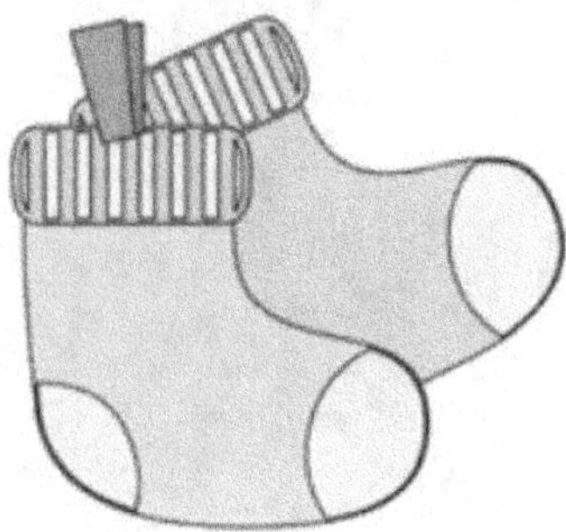

My baby sister wears socks.

costume

garnitur

My brother is wearing a suit.

chandail

sweter

I am wearing a sweater for winter.

cravate

krawat

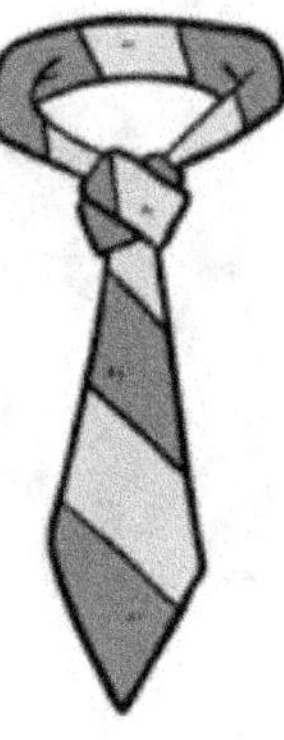

My dad wears a tie to meetings.

pantalon

spodnie

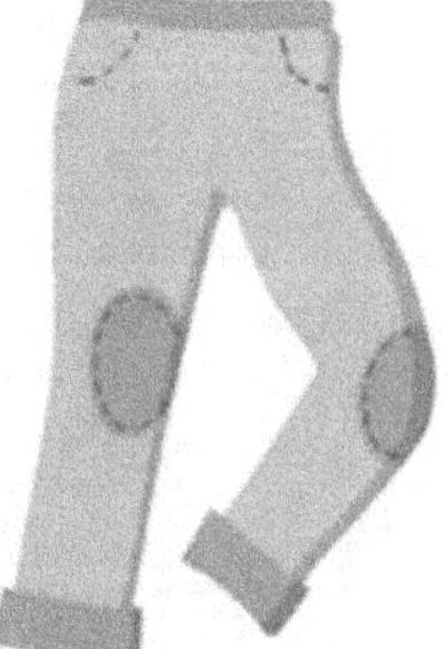

The trousers look like jeans.

slip

slipy

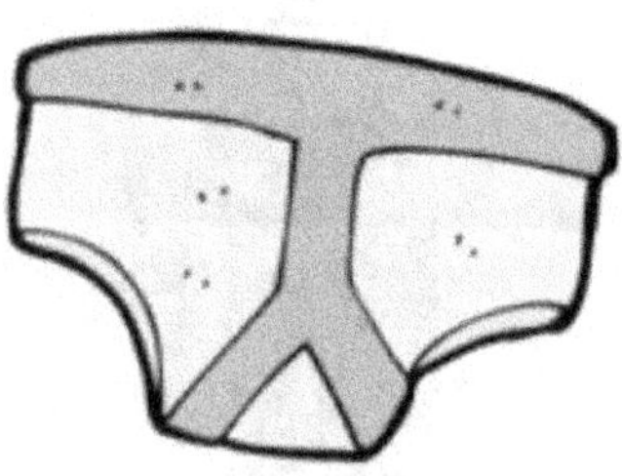

I always wear my underwear.

maillot de corps

podkoszulek

My undershirt has a star.

une

jeden

Number one and the bee are friends.

deux

dwa

The cat and the mouse both love two.

trois

trzy

The bear gives number three a present.

quatre

cztery

Number four is a home for the cat.

cinq

pięć

Number five hatches an egg.

six

sześć

Number six is going to eat a carrot.

sept

siedem

Number seven is playing with the tiger.

huit

osiem

Number eight is funny.

neuf

dziewięć

Number nine meets the parrot.

dix

dziesięć

Number ten is smiling.

onze

jedenaście

Number eleven has big eyes.

douze

dwanaście

Number twelve is number one and two.

treize

trzynaście

Number thirteen is excited.

quatorze

czternaście

The number fourteen is vast.

quinze

piętnaście

The number fifteen is green.

seize

szesnaście

Sixteen is my lucky number.

dix-sept

siedemnaście

Number seventeen look alike.

dix-huit

osiemnaście

Number eighteen will go to the circus.

dix-neuf

dziewiętnaście

I am nineteen now!

vingt

20

Number twenty has a zero.

fourmi

mrówka

The ant has lots of legs.

cloche

dzwon

The bell will ring.

vache

krowa

The cow has a bow.

poupée

lalka

She has a cute bear doll.

oeuf

jajko

The chick has hatched out of the egg.

poisson

ryba

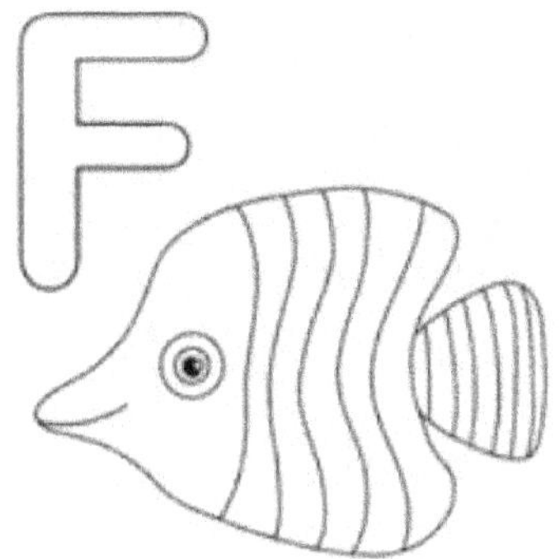

The fish is swimming in the water.

chèvre

koza

The goat is sitting on the grass.

chapeau

kapelusz

He is wearing a hat.

crème glacée

lody

I like to eat ice cream.

confiture

dżem

The kitten is sitting on the jam jar.

chaton

kotek

The cat is sleeping on the floor.

lion

lew

The lion is waiting for the tiger.

rat

szczur

The mouse has lots of presents.

nez

nos

The reindeer has a red nose.

hibou

sowa

The owl is sleeping.

porc

śwnia...

The pig will eat cupcakes.

reine

królowa

The queen has a big crown.

lapin

królik

The rabbit is jumping up and down.

mouton

owca

The sheep have fluffy wool.

tortue

żółw

The turtle has a shell.

parapluie

parasol

The mouse is holding an umbrella.

van

awangarda

The van is driving along the road.

pastèque

arbuz

The watermelon has lots of seeds.

xylophone

ksylofon

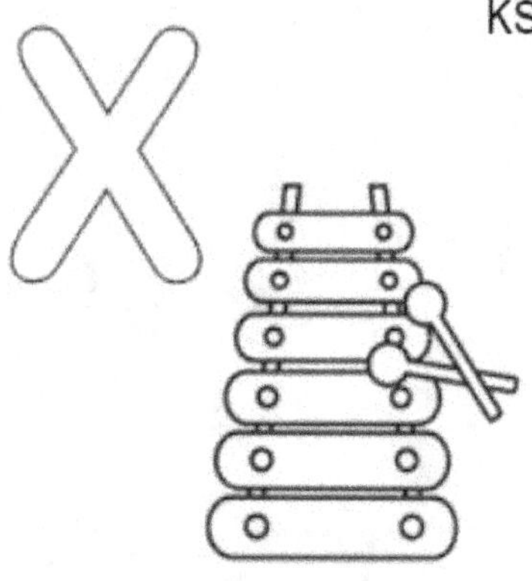

We are going to play the
xylophone.

yaourt

jogurt

We opened the yogurt can.

zèbre

zebra

The zebra is surprised.

rose

różowy

color the word and
the picture in pink

Most of my clothes are pink.

marron

brązowy

color the word and
the picture in pink

brown

My chocolate is brown.

gris
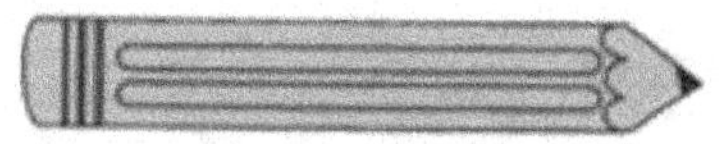

szary

color the word and
the picture in pink

gray

I don't like the color gray.

vert

zielony

color the word and
the picture in pink

green

The vegetables are green.

jaune

żółty

color the word and
the picture in pink

yellow

Bananas are yellow.

blanc

biały

color the word and
the picture in pink

white

The paper that I write on is white.

rouge

czerwony

color the word and
the picture in pink

red

Apples are red.

bleu

niebieski

color the word and
the picture in pink

The night sky is blue.

percer

wiercić

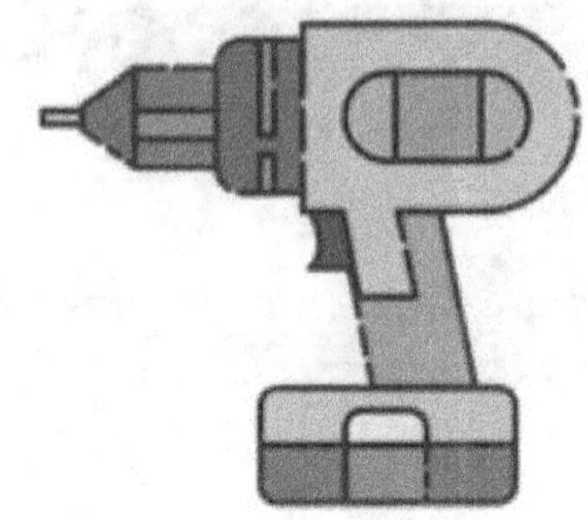

The drill will help us fix this.

marteau

młotek

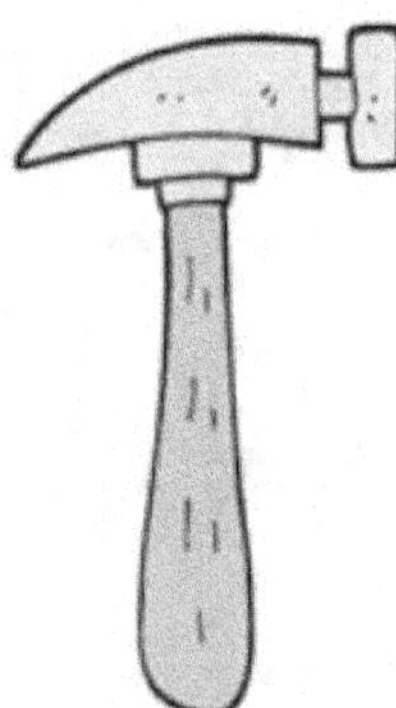

The hammer is going to nail the
picture.

couteau

nóż

The knife is sharp.

pinces

szczypce

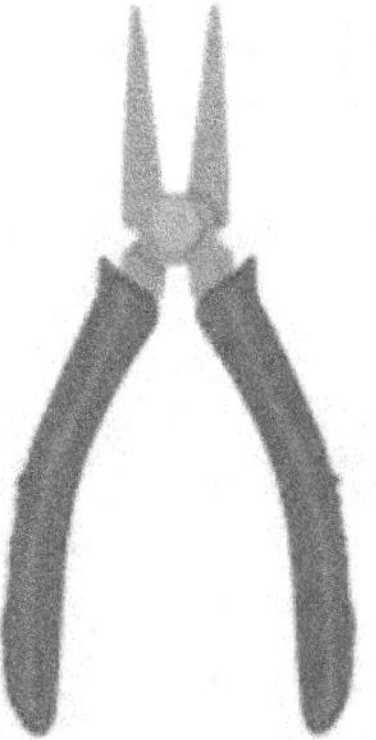

The plier is used for many things.

vu

piła

The saw can chop wood.

les ciseaux

nożyce

I use scissors to cut paper.

tournevis

śrubokręt

The screwdriver can screw in the knots.

clé

klucz

The wrench can help unscrew the knots.

avion

samolot

The airplane is going to leave now.

vélo

rower

The bicycle is beautiful.

bateau

łódź

The boat is floating on the water.

autobus

autobus

The bus is going to school.

voiture

samochód

The car is green.

hélicoptère

śmigłowiec

The helicopter is looking for something.

cheval

koń

You can ride the horse.

jet

strumień

The jet is high-speed.

moto

motocykl

The motorcycle is on the road.

navire

statek

The ship is on the water.

métro

metro

My mom goes on the subway to work.

taxi

taxi

The taxi has someone inside.

train

pociąg

The train is going slowly.

un camion

samochód ciężarowy

The truck has stuff in it.

asperges

szparag

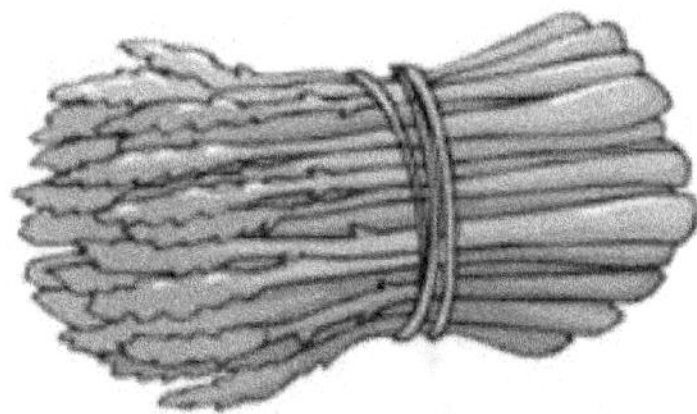

The asparagus is in a bundle.

des haricots

fasolki

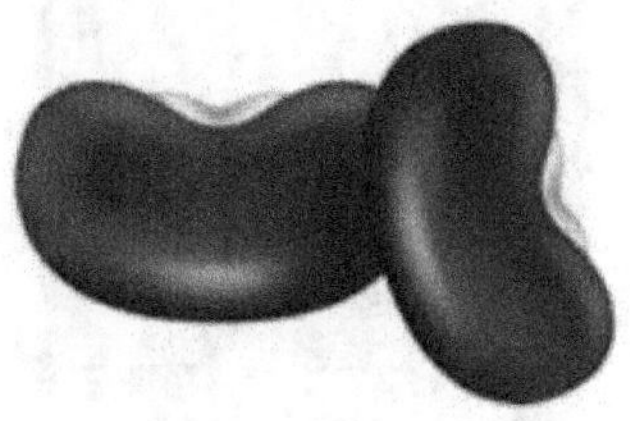

The beans are smooth.

brocoli

brokuły

The broccoli is dancing.

chou

kapusta

Bunnies like to eat cabbage.

carotte

marchewka

The carrots are very long.

céleri

seler

The celery has lots of leaves.

blé

kukurydza

Corn soup is delicious.

concombre

ogórek

The cucumbers are cut into pieces.

aubergine

bakłażan

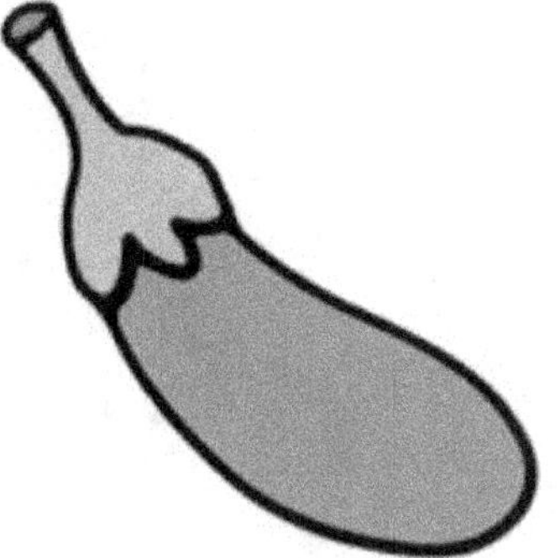

The eggplant is purple.

poivre vert

zielony pieprz

The green pepper is juicy.

salade

sałata

The lettuce is all green.

oignon

cebula

The onions make my eyes water.

pois

groszek

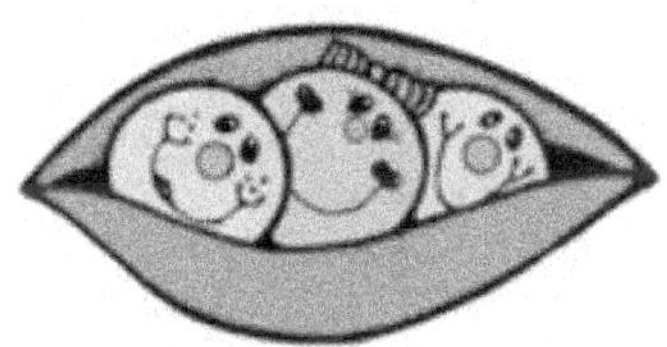

The peas are all in a pod.

patate

ziemniak

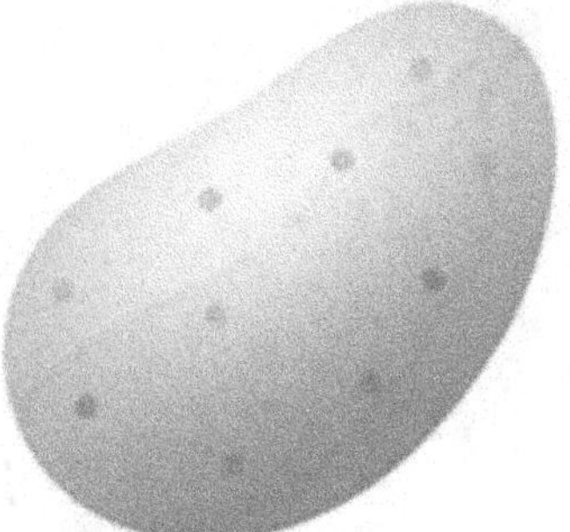

The potato is very shiny.

citrouille

dynia

The pumpkin is for Halloween.

un radis

rzodkiewka

The radish is a type of vegetable.

épinard

szpinak

The spinach is good with cheese.

patate douce

słodki ziemniak

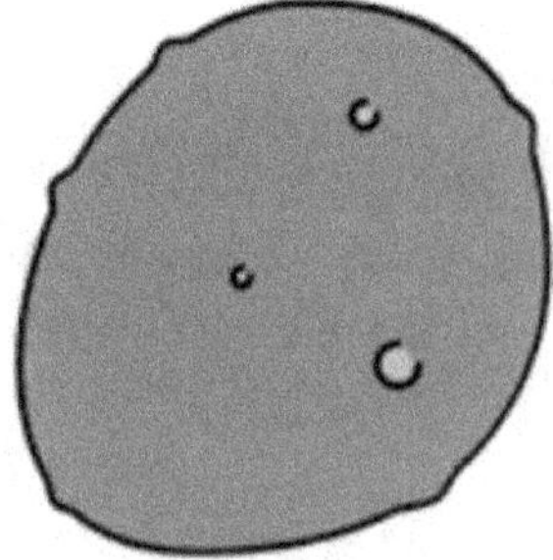

The sweet potato is quite sweet.

tomate

pomidor

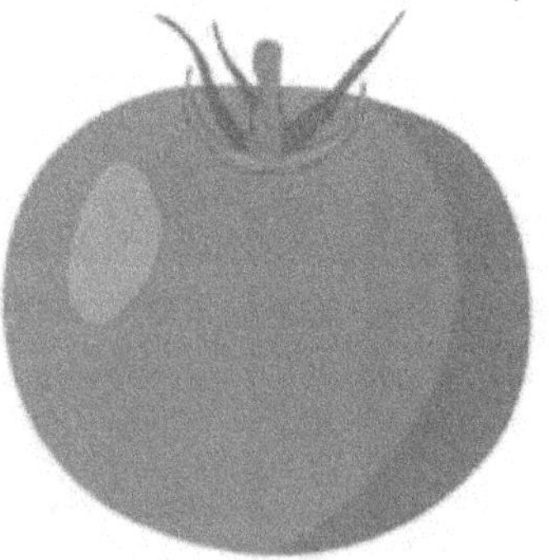

I don't like to eat tomatoes.

navet

rzepa

My mom bought some turnips.

nuageux

pochmurny

The weather is cloudy today.

du froid

zimno

I like cold weather.

cool

chłodny

The temperature is cold today.

brumeux

mglisty

The fog is so strong I can't see the city.

chaud

gorąco

The fire is burning hot.

humide

wilgotny

It's so humid and wet today.

pluvieux

deszczowy

It's raining very hard.

neigeux

śnieżny

Welcome to snow land!

orageux

burzliwy

I hate the stormy weather.

ensoleillé

słoneczny

The sun is shining!

chaud

ciepły

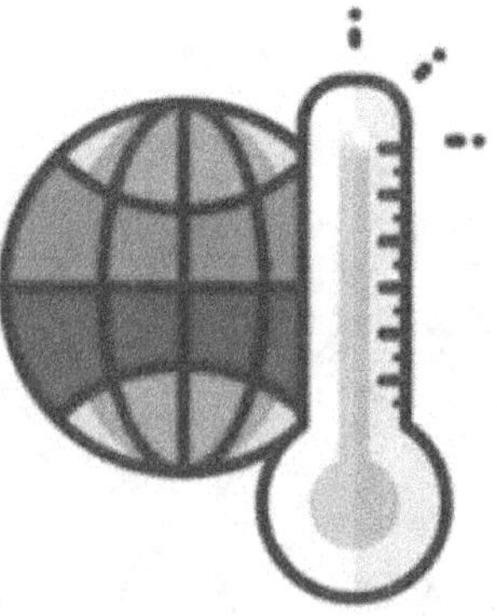

The whole world is warm today!

venteux

wietrzny

The leaves are blowing away since it's so windy!

tante

ciocia

My aunt is very nice to me.

frère

brat

My brother is very fun to play with.

cousin

kuzyn

I love going to the playground with my cousin.

fille

córka

I like to read books with my daughter.

père

ojciec

My father is playing with me.

petite fille

wnuczka

My granddaughter has blond hair.

grand-mère

babcia

My grandmother is very old and has glasses.

petit fils

wnuk

My grandson and I are very excited today!

mère

matka

My mother likes to pick me up.

neveu

bratanek

My father's nephew is my cousin.

nièce

siostrzenica

My niece is very good at playing ball.

sœur

siostra

My sister is so pretty!

fils

syn

My son likes to play with toy cars.

belle fille

pasierbica

My stepdaughter likes the color orange.

belle-mère

macocha

My stepmother is pretty.

beau-fils

pasierb

This is my stepson, Greg.

oncle

wujek

My uncle tells lots of funny jokes.

bol

miska

The bowl has nothing inside.

tasse

puchar

My mom drinks her coffee out of a cup.

plat

danie

That dish has a bone inside.

fourchette

widelec

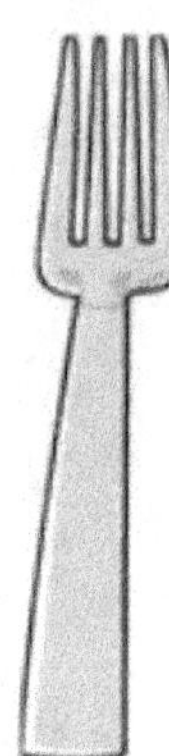

We have more spoons than forks.

verre

szkło

I have a glass of water on my desk.

couteau

nóż

I have a knife in my kitchen.

agresser

kubek

This mug of coffee is for my dad.

serviette de table

serwetka

You can use the napkins to clean your hands.

poivre

pieprz

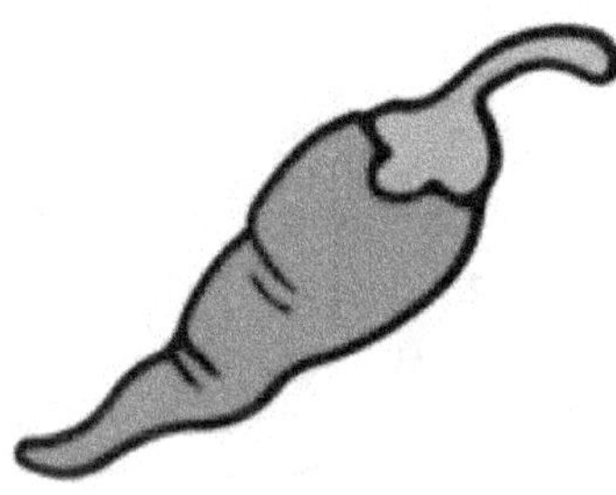

The pepper is very spicy.

lanceur

dzban

Pour yourself some lemonade from the pitcher.

assiette

talerz

Can you help me wash the plates?

salade

sałatka

The salad is very healthy for you.

sel

sól

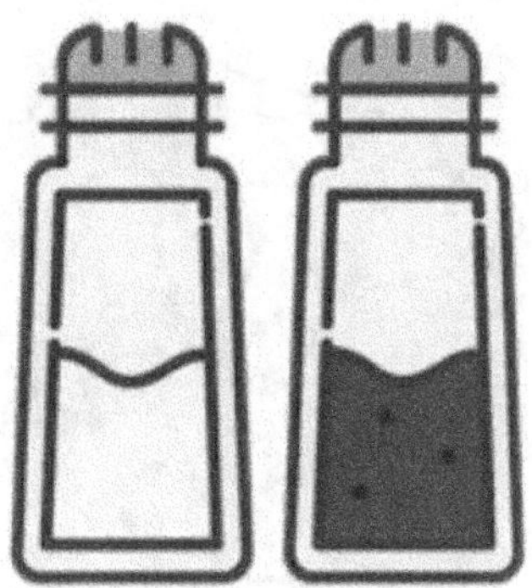

The salt tastes good with a few pinches of pepper.

soucoupe

spodek

The plate is for my cup.

cuillère

łyżka

I use a spoon to eat my rice.

sucre

cukier

The pack of sugar is very heavy.

dimanche

niedziela

Sunday

Sunday is the day to go to Church!

lundi

poniedziałek

Monday

Monday is the day to start school.

mardi

wtorek

Tuesday

We will go to the shops on Tuesday.

mercredi

środa

Wednesday

Wednesday is hard to spell!

jeudi

czwartek

Thursday

Thursday is the fourth day of the week!

vendredi

piątek

Friday

My birthday is on Friday!

samedi

sobota

Saturday

Saturday is the weekend!

cuire

piec

The chef will bake a cake.

ébullition

gotować

I will boil the eggs.

griller

burda

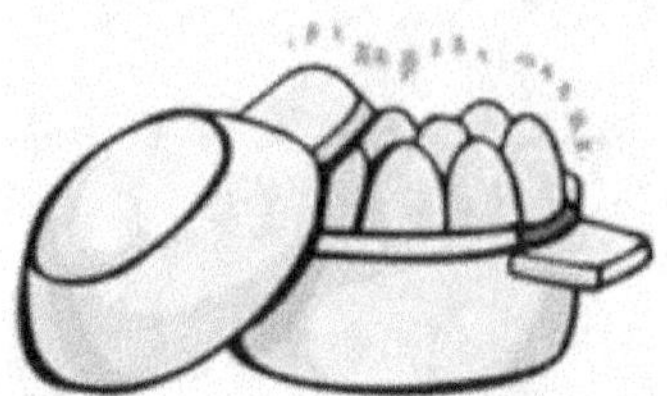

Broil is very yummy.

ouvre-boîte

otwieracz do puszek

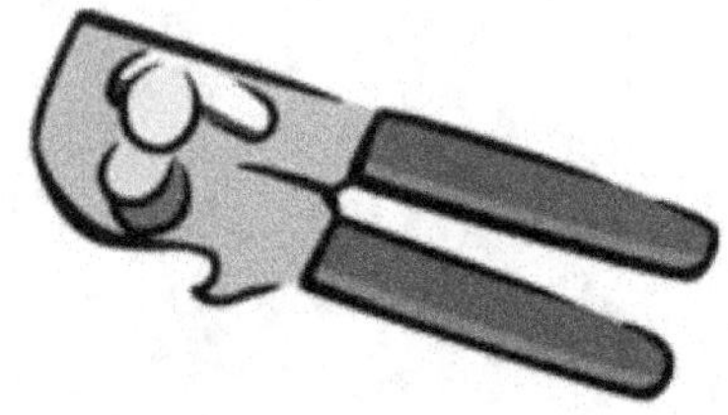

That can opener is used for
opening cans.

frire

smażyć

The pan can fry lots of things.

gril

grill

We have a grill in our backyard.

tasse à mesurer

miarka

My mom uses the measuring cup
for baking.

cuillère à mesurer

miarka

I use a measuring spoon to eat my dessert.

four micro onde

kuchenka mikrofalowa

The microwave is used to heat food.

bol à mélanger

misa miksująca

She is using the mixing bowl to mix things.

serviettes en papier

ręczniki papierowe

Dry your hands with paper towels.

poché aux œufs

jajko w koszulce

The poach is put on noodles.

porte pot

uchwyt na garnek

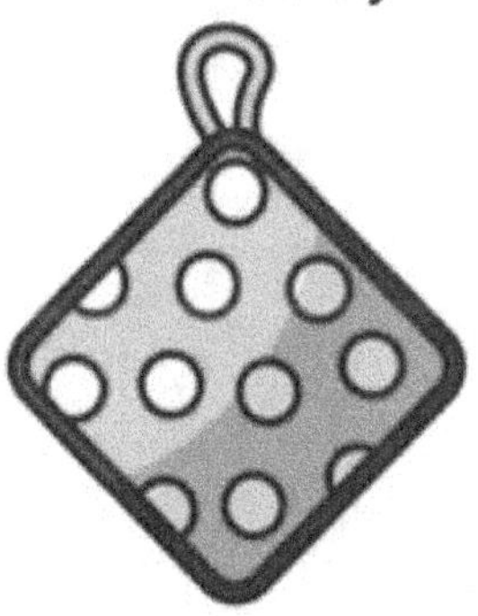

The potholder is soft.

rôti

pi`eczeń`

The chef made roast chicken.

rouleau à pâtisserie

wałek do ciasta

He is holding a rolling pin.

brouiller

wdrapywać się

My mom is making scrambled eggs for breakfast.

mijoter

dusić

The simmer is rice today.

couteau

nóż

The knife is sharp.

cuillère

łyżka

I eat my food with a spoon and fork.

spatule

szpachelka

The spatula will help us flip the steak over.

vapeur

parowy

The steam is coming from the pot.

passoire

filtr

The strainer is used to strain stuff.

minuteur

regulator czasowy

I set my timer for 12:00.

fourchette

widelec

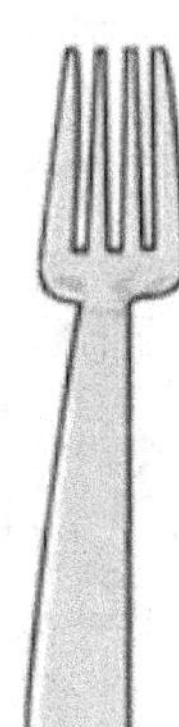

I have lots of metallic forks.

grille-pain

opiekacz

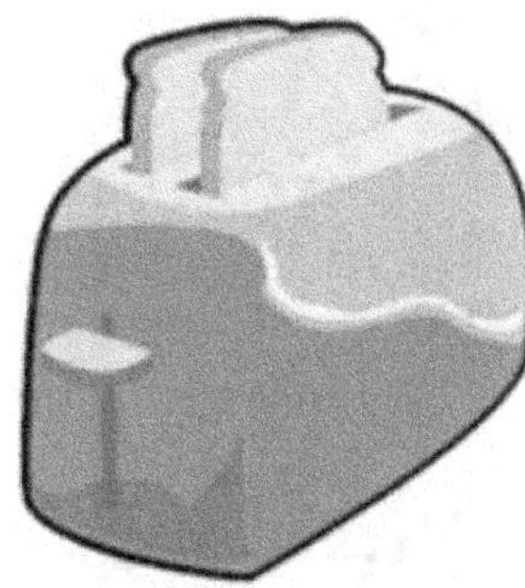

The toaster will toast my bread.

bouilloire

czajnik

The kettle has tea inside.

réfrigérateur

lodówka

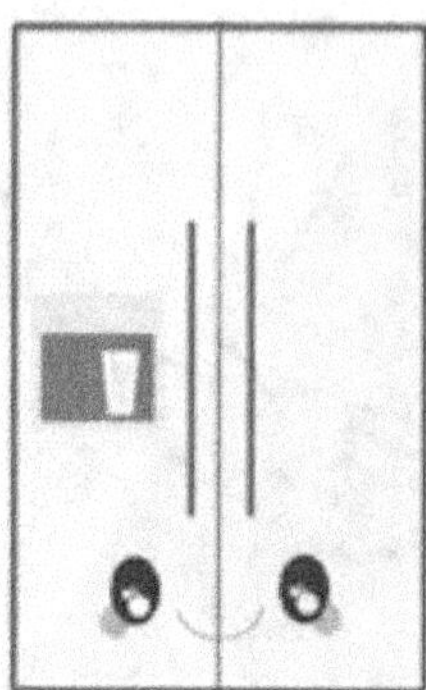

The refrigerator has lots of things inside.

mixeur

mikser

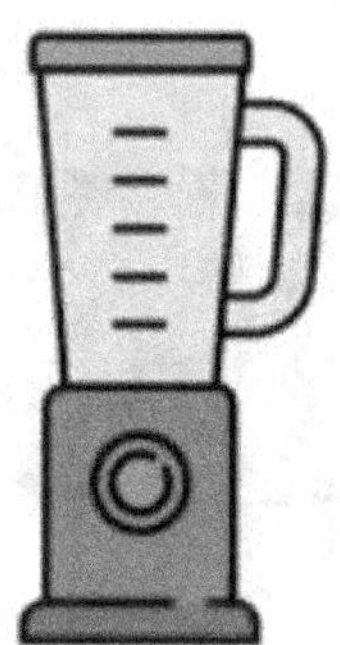

The blender will mix up my fruits.

cabinets

szafki

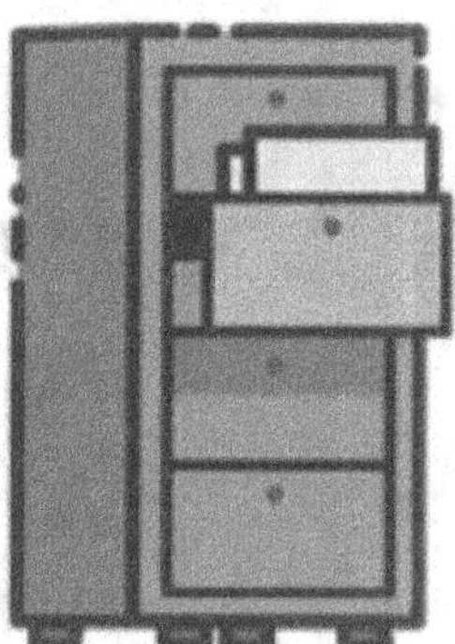

The cabinet has my paper inside.

placard

kredens

The cupboard has lots of books.

four micro onde

kuchenka mikrofalowa

The microwave will heat my food.

arrière

plecy

She has a slender back.

des joues

policzki

She kisses her mom on the cheek.

poitrine

klatka piersiowa

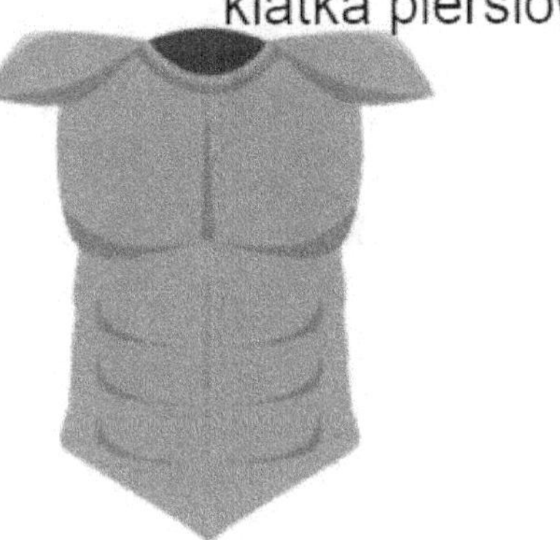

The armor is for your chest.

menton

broda

This is my chin!

oreilles

uszy

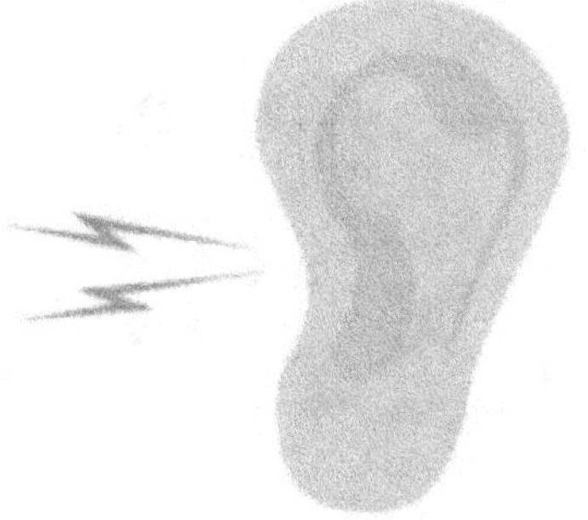

The ear is hearing something.

les sourcils

brwi

The eyebrows are raised.

yeux

oczy

The eyes are blue.

pieds

stopy

I have one pair of feet.

des doigts

palce

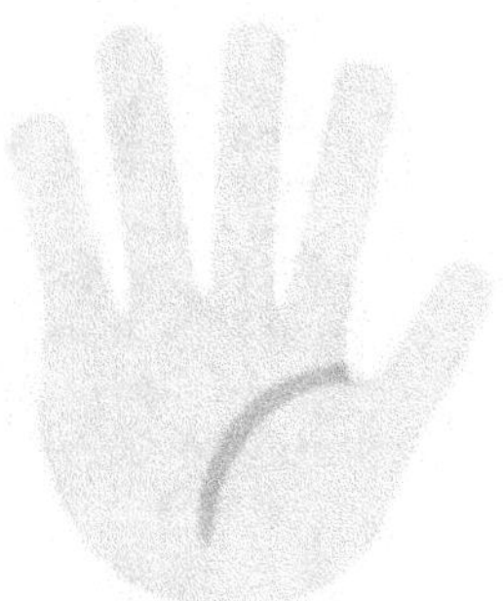

The fingers are waving at us.

pied

stopa

My foot has five fingers.

front

czoło

My brain is behind my forehead.

cheveux

włosy

My hair is long and black.

mains

ręce

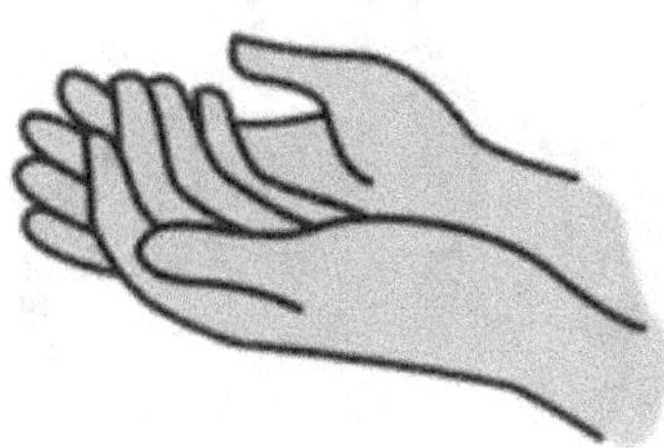

I will wash my hands in the sink.

tête

głowa

She has a big head.

les hanches

biodra

The gorilla has his hands on his hips.

les genoux

kolana

She is begging on her knees.

jambes

nogi

The tiger has strong legs.

lèvres

usta

The lips have lipstick on.

bouche

usta

He is covering his mouth with his hand.

cou

szyja

The necklace is very special to me.

nez

nos

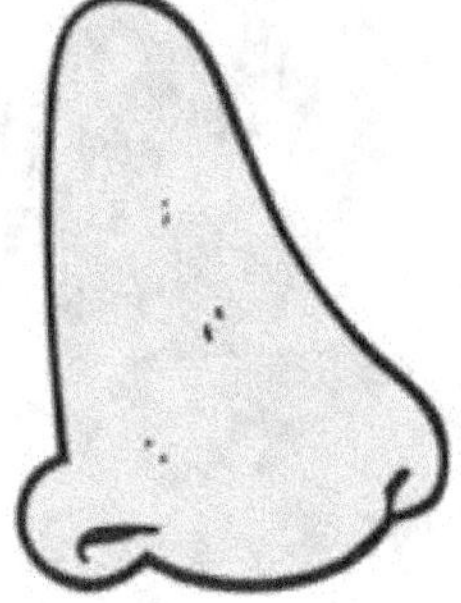

The nose smells something.

épaules

ramiona

He puts his hands on his shoulders.

estomac

żołądek

He has a big stomach.

les dents

zęby

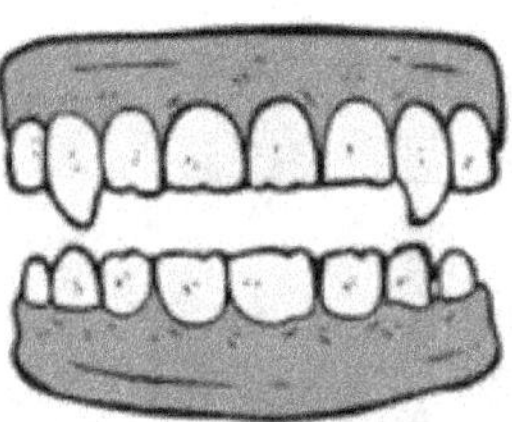

The teeth are clean and white.

gorge

gardło

He has a sore throat today.

les orteils

palce u stóp

My toes are small.

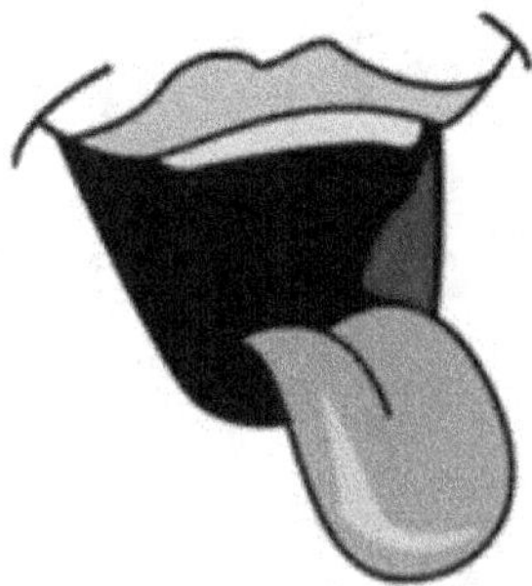

langue

język

My tongue is licking ice cream.

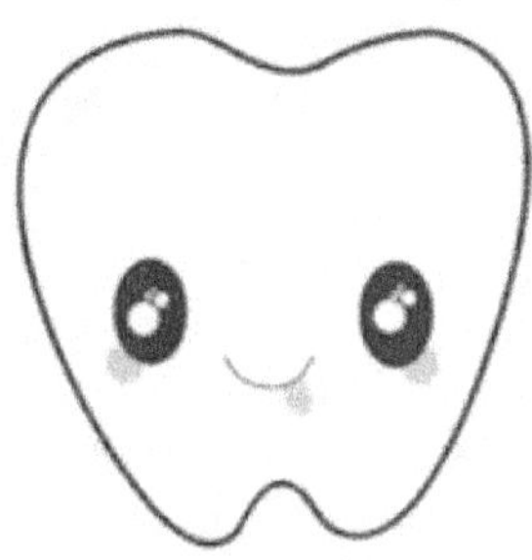

dent

ząb

The tooth has big eyes.

taille

talia

He has his hands on his waist.

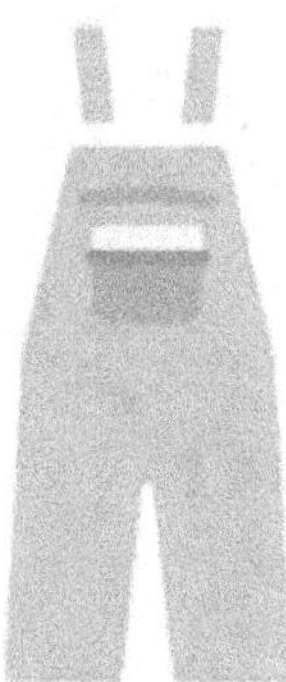

salopette

kombinezon

I bought these overalls for you!

mitaines

rękawice

The mittens are very warm.

bonnet

czapka bez daszka

The beanie is for winter.

tablier

fartuch

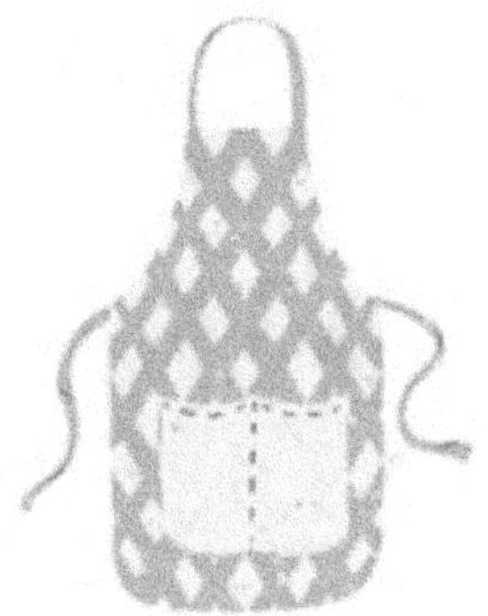

I wear my apron when I bake.

poupée

lalka

The doll is for my baby sister.

hochets

grzechotki

The rattle is for the baby.

jouet

zabawka

The toy is very fun.

couche

pielucha

The baby has to wear a diaper.

berceau

kołyska pleciona

She is sleeping in her bassinet.

bavoir

śliniaczek

My baby brother has to wear his
bib when he is eating.

octogone

ośmiokąt

The octagon is saying okay!

triangle

trójkąt

The triangle has three corners.

carré

plac

Square

The square has four sides.

cercle

okrąg

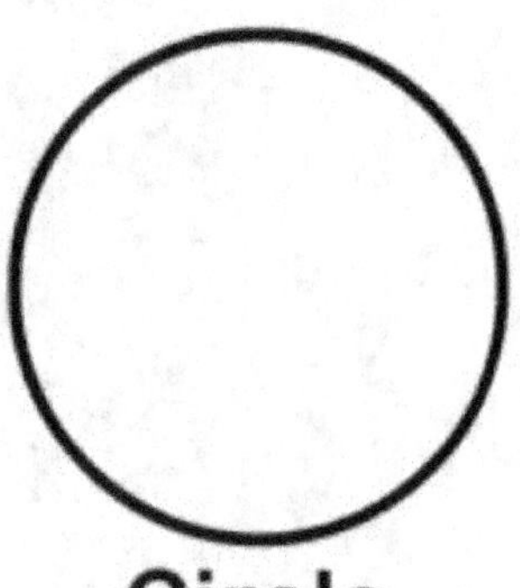

Circle

The circle is round.

ovale

owalny

The oval shape looks like a circle.

cœur

serce

I drew a heart on my paper.

traverser

krzyż

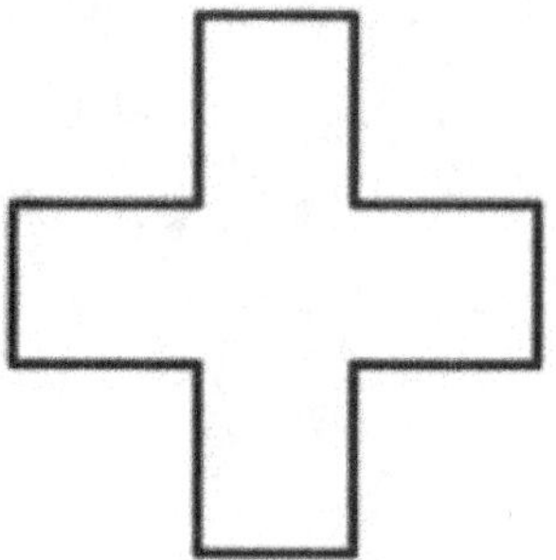

That sign is a cross.

la flèche

strzałka

The arrow is pointing this way.

cube

sześcian

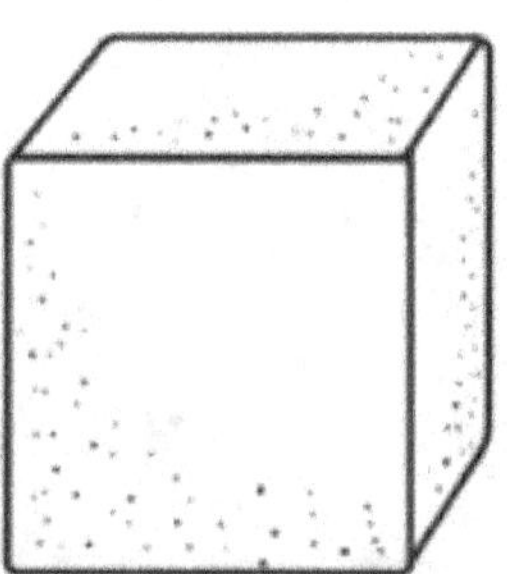

The cube is 3D.

étoile

gwiazda

The star is yellow and shiny.

tir à l'arc

łucznictwo

The archery is where you aim.

badminton

badminton

My favorite sport is badminton.

criquet

krykiet

I am very good at cricket.

bowling

kręgle

I got one pin down at bowling!

boxe

boks

The boxing gloves are hot.

tennis

tenis ziemny

He can hit the ball in tennis.

faire de la planche à roulettes

jazda na deskorolce

He skateboards to school.

planche de surf

deska surfingowa

The shark loves surfing in the ocean.

le hockey

hokej

I like to play Ice hockey.

yoga

joga

He is closing his eyes and doing yoga.

épée

szermierka

They are fencing and dueling together.

aptitude

zdatność

She will do some fitness in the pool.

gymnastique

gimnastyka

He can do brilliant gymnastics.

karaté

karate

She is good at kicking in Karate.

volley-ball

siatkówka

She is holding a volleyball.

musculation

podnoszenie ciężarów

The girl with brown hair can do weightlifting.

basketball

koszykówka

He can balance the ball with one finger in basketball.

base-ball

baseball

The little chick is in the finales at baseball.

le rugby

rugby

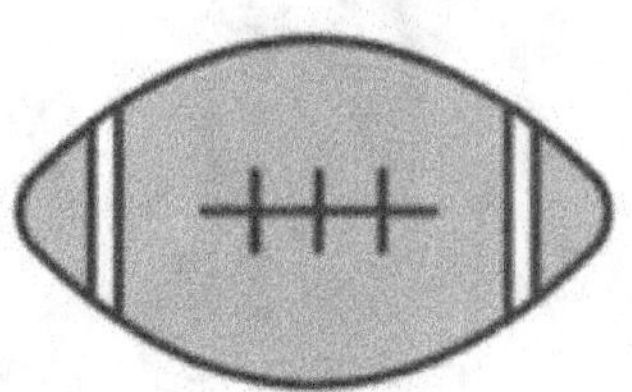

The rugby ball has white stripes.

lutte

zapasy

The sumo will compete in wrestling.

course de voitures

samochód wyścigowy

He is number one for car racing.

cyclisme

jazda rowerem

He is peacefully cycling on the road.

fonctionnement

bieganie

He is running while listening to his earphones.

tennis de table

tenis stołowy

My brother and dad will play table tennis.

pêche

wędkarstwo

He will go to the river to fish.

judo

dżudo

She has a red belt in Judo.

escalade

wspinaczka

He will climb the ladder.

tournage

strzelanie

He is shooting the archery board.

le golf

golf

She is going to compete in the golf competition.

balade

jazda

He will ride his scooter.

asseyez-vous

usiądź

They are sitting down together.

se lever

wstań

She likes to stand up.

bats toi

walka

They are fighting over the book.

rire

śmiech

He is laughing so hard!

lis

czytać

She read a picture book.

jouer

grać

He went to play on the slide.

ecoutez

słuchać

He listened for the ice cream cart.

pleurer

płakać

He cried because he got a bad grade.

pense

myśleć

He thought that the test would be hard.

chanter

śpiewać

He sang for the concert.

regarder la télévision

oglądać telewizję

He watched TV the whole night.

danse

taniec

She was a good dancer.

allumer

włączyć

The light is turned on.

éteindre

wyłączyć

The light is turned off.

gagner

zdobyć

He won the contest.

mouche

latać

The parrot can fly.

couper

skaleczenie

He was cutting his nails.

désinvolte

wyrzucić

He threw away the garbage.

dormir

spać

He slept soundly.

fermer

blisko

He closed his mouth shut.

ouvert

otwarty

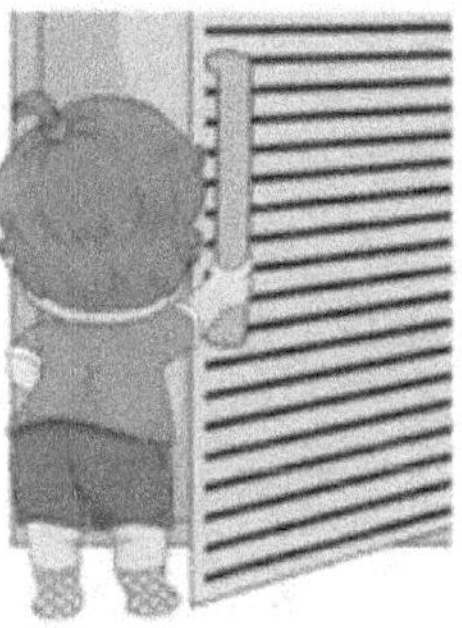

She opened the bathroom door.

écrire

pisać

She wrote with a pencil.

donner

dać

Santa gave her a present.

sauter

skok

She had fun jumping.

manger

jeść

The shark ate yummy ice cream.

boisson

drink

The old British man drank tea.

cuisinier

gotować

The microwave cooked his soup.

lavage

myć się

You need to remember to wash your hands.

attendre

czekać

He was waiting for the bus.

montée

wspinać się

She climbed a lot of mountains.

parler

rozmowa

Two best friends were talking together.

crawl

czołgać się

The baby crawled on the floor.

rêver

śnić

The Sloth dreamed about eating leaves.

creuser

kopać

That strong man dug a swimming pool.

taper

klaskać

The baby clapped her hands.

tricoter

robić na drutach

She knits with the purple string.

coudre

szyć

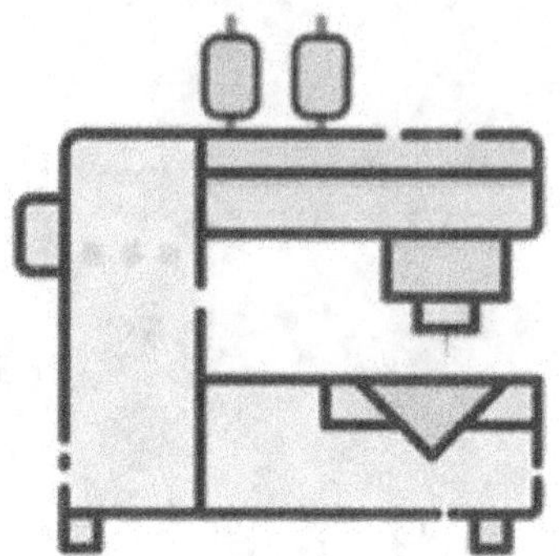

That is a sewing machine.

odeur

zapach

The perfume smelled great.

baiser

pocałunek

He kissed his mother.

étreinte

przytulić

They hugged each other.

ronfler

chrapać

The tiger snored.

baigner

kąpać się

He took a bath.

s'incliner

kłaniając się

He bowed to the judge.

peindre

farba

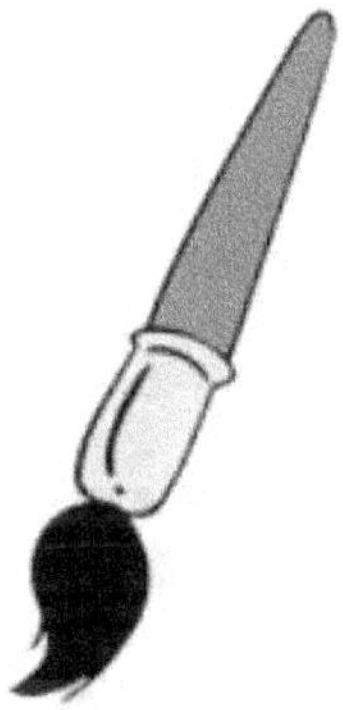

He painted a colorful picture.

se plonger

nurkować

He dove to the deepest part of the ocean.

ski

narty

The ski was expensive.

empiler

stos

The books are stacked high.

acheter

kup

They bought cereal.

secouer

potrząsnąć

They shook hands together.

programmeur

programista

He was a smart computer programmer.

vétérinaire

lekarz weterynarii

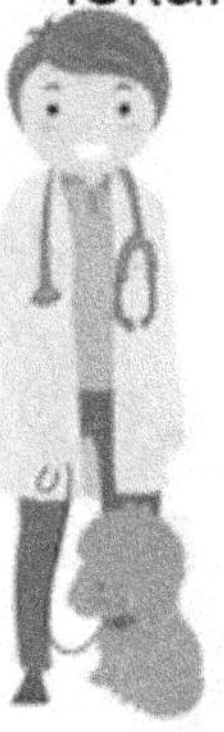

She is a veterinarian.

vendeur de rue

uliczny sprzedawca

That street vendor sells hot dogs.

mineur

górnik

That Miner will find gold.

prof

nauczyciel

The owl is the teacher.

groom

goniec hotelowy

That Bellboy is fat.

orateur

głośnik

The chicken is a great Speaker.

boucher

rzeźnik

The Butcher sells fish.

pharmacien

farmaceuta

That Pharmacist saved a person's life.

réceptionniste

recepcjonista

He is a Receptionist.

politicien

polityk

He wants to be a Politician.

guide touristique

przewodnik wycieczki

That Tour guide led us around Japan.

entrepreneur

przedsiębiorca

He is an Entrepreneur.

danseuse de ballet

tancerz baletowy

She is training to be a Ballet dancer.

astronaute

astronauta

He is a great astronaut.

juge

sędzia

That Judge is always fair.

avocat

prawnik

The lawyer is serious.

la caissière

kasjer

She is a cashier at the market.

conducteur de taxi

kierowca taksówki

He is a fast Taxi driver.

plombier

hydraulik

That Plumber fixes toilets.

musicien

muzyk

She wants to be a Musician like her teacher.

chef

szef kuchni

The chef makes fast food.

boulanger

piekarz

That baker is a bread.

artiste

artysta

That Artist came from Italy.

acteur

aktor

That actor is famous.

barman

barman

The Bartender works in a bar.

coiffeur

fryzjer

That girl is a Hairdresser.

évêques

biskupi

He is a Bishop.

opticien

optyk

She went to an Optician.

fleuriste

kwiaciarz

She is a great Florist.

écrivain

pisarz

He is a famous author.

comptable

księgowy

My accountant is loyal.

du vin

wino

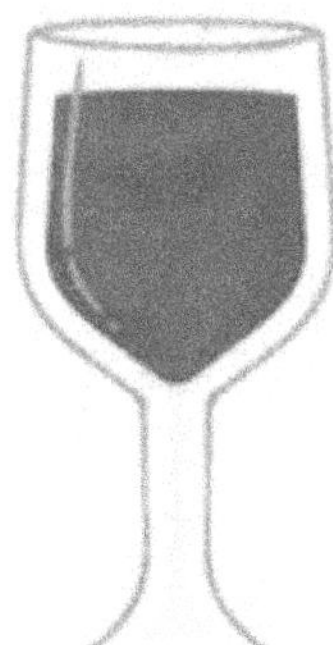

That wine tastes good.

café

kawa

That coffee is bitter.

limonade

lemoniada

The lemonade is refreshing.

chocolat chaud

gorąca czekolada

I drink hot chocolate every day.

milk-shake

napój mleczny

The milkshake has whipped cream.

eau

woda

The water is not cold.

thé

herbata

The tea is hot.

lait

mleko

Milk is white.

bière

piwo

The beer is foamy.

un soda

soda

The soda is fizzy.

smoothie

koktajl

The smoothie is a watermelon flavor.

milk-shake

napój mleczny

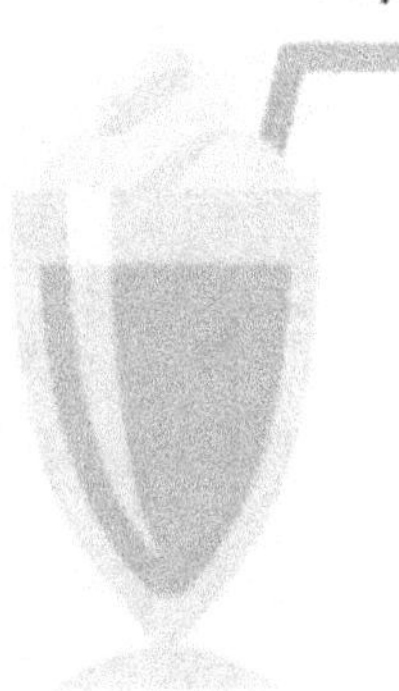

The milkshake has whipped cream.

lait de coco

mleko kokosowe

The coconut milk is yummy.

du jus d'orange

sok pomarańczowy

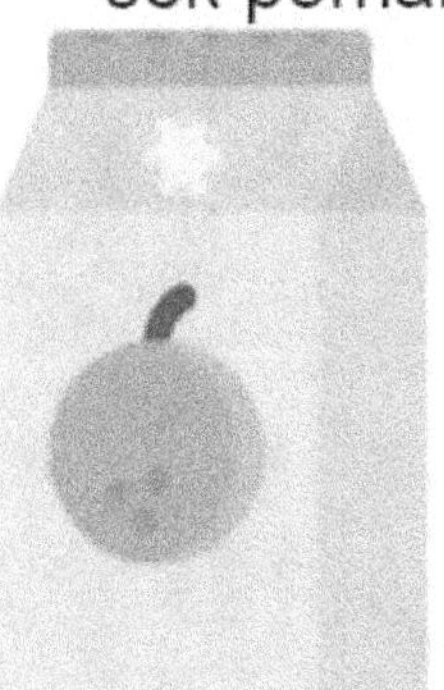

The orange juice is made from oranges.

cacao

kakao

The cocoa is sweet.

fromage

ser

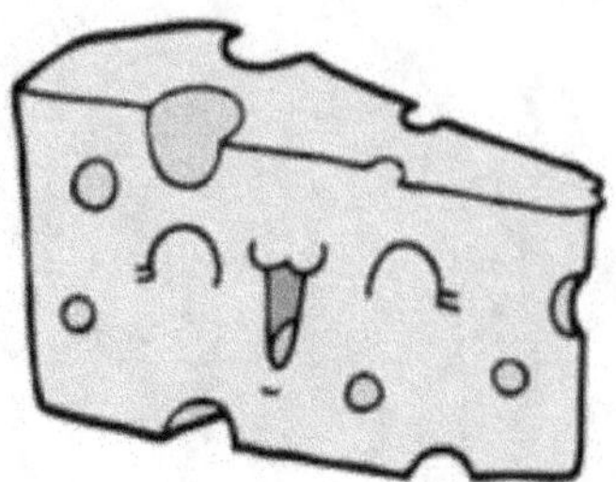

The cheese is creamy.

oeuf

jajko

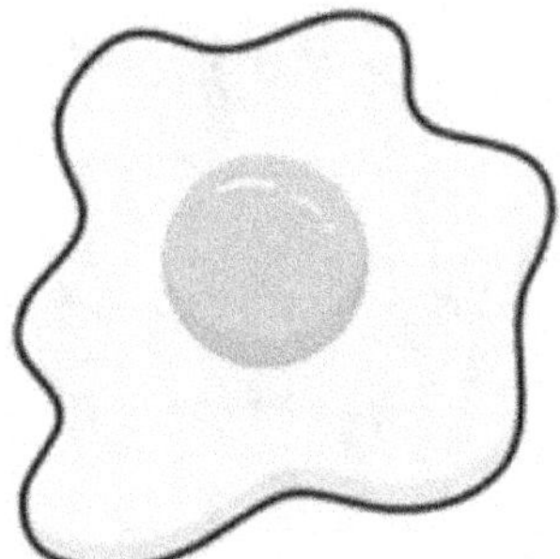

The egg is fried.

beurre

masło

The butter is put on bread.

margarine

margaryna

Margarine looks like butter.

yaourt

jogurt

That yogurt is popular.

cottage cheese

twarożek

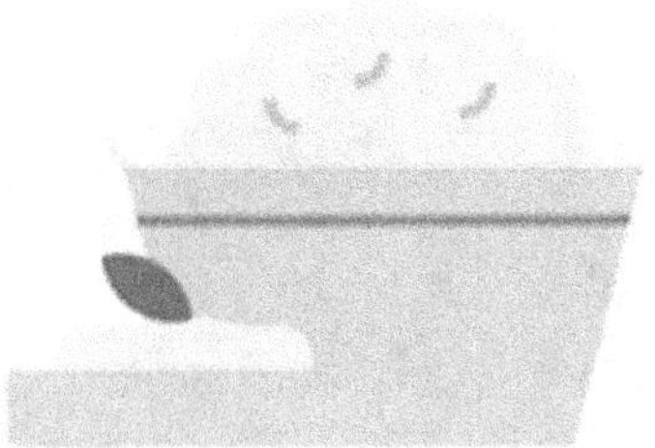

The cottage cheese is put on crackers.

crème glacée

lody

They have a triple scoop ice cream.

crème

krem

That is a lot of creams.

sandwich

kanapka

That sandwich is healthy.

saucisse

kiełbasa

Americans love sausages.

hamburger

hamburger

That hamburger looks happy.

hot-dog

hot dog

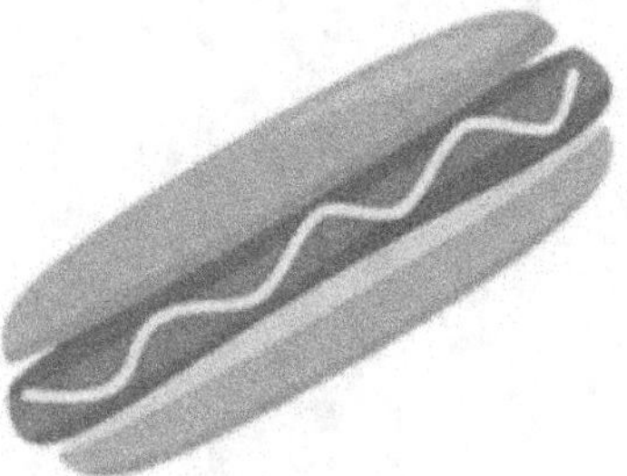

That hot dog has mustard on it.

pain

chleb

That bread is saying hello.

pizza

pizza

That pizza is cheesy.

steak

stek

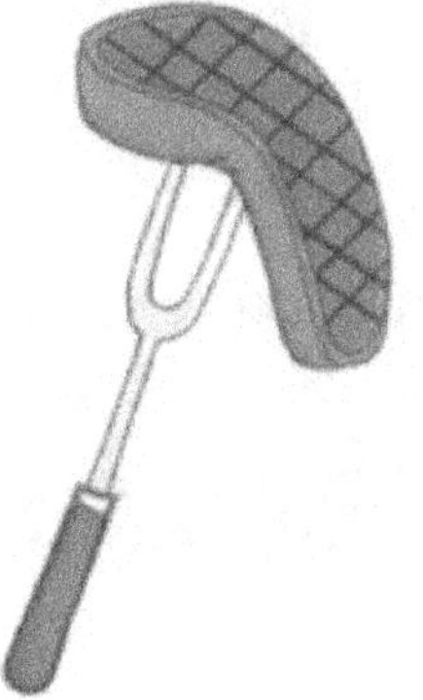

The steak was grilled.

poulet rôti

pieczony kurczak

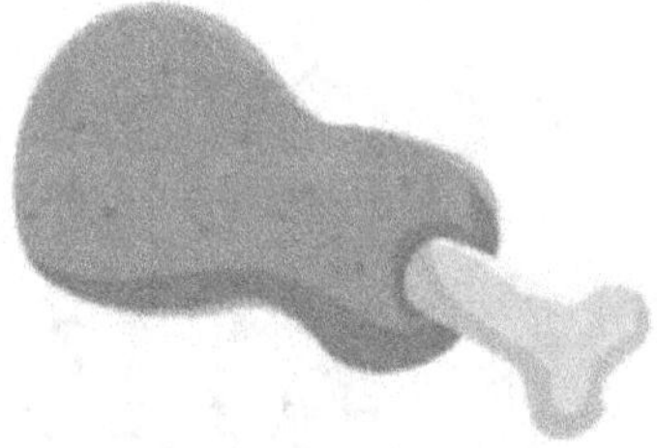

Roast Chicken is delicious.

poisson

ryba

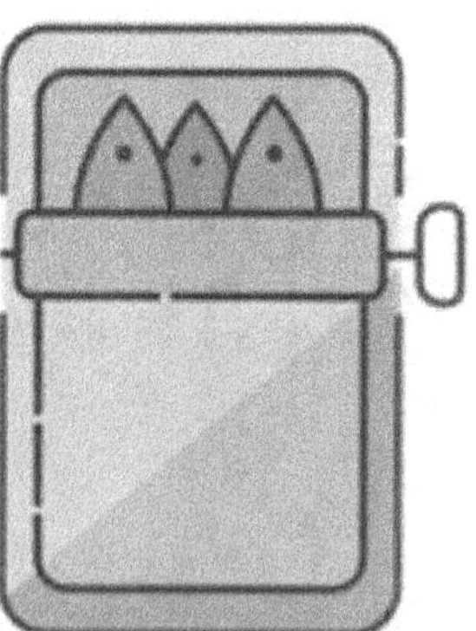

You can buy canned fish in the market.

fruit de mer

owoce morza

Lobster is expensive seafood.

jambon

szynka

Ham can be put in sandwiches.

kebab

kebab

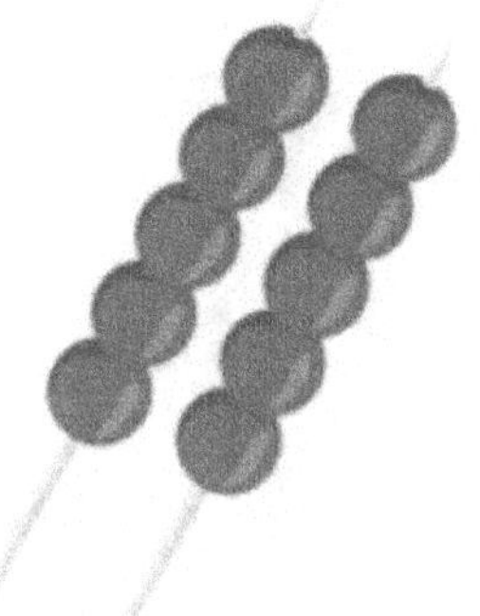

Kebab is a delicacy in America.

bacon

boczek

That bacon is smiling.

crème fraîche

kwaśna śmietana

You can dip your chips in sour cream.

vache

krowa

Cows are black and white.

lapin

królik

That rabbit is fun to play with.

canard

kaczka

That duck is content.

crevette

krewetka

The shrimp has six legs.

porc

świnia

That pig is pink and fat.

abeille

pszczoła

The bee has a stinger.

chèvre

koza

That goat has a white horn.

crabe

krab

The crab has two big pincers.

cerf

jeleń

That deer is sleeping.

dinde

indyk

The turkey has a giant tail.

colombe

gołąb

That dove is carrying a plant.

mouton

owca

That sheep has fluffy wool.

poisson

ryba

That fish has colorful fins.

poulet

kurczak

That chicken is waking everybody up.

cheval

koń

The horse has a red mane.

chaise

krzesło

That wing chair is yellow.

meuble tv

stojak tv

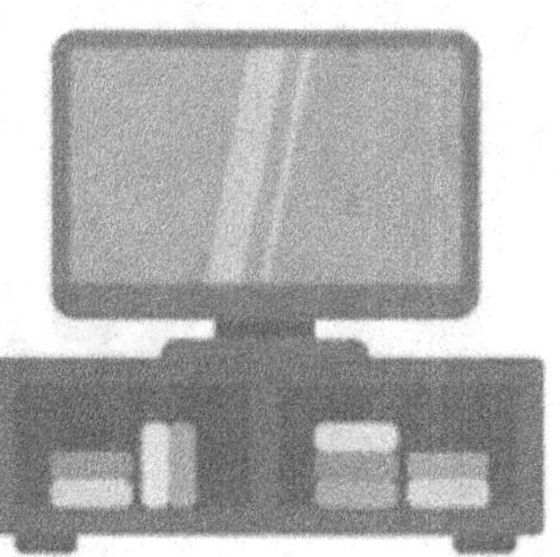

The TV stand can hold books.

canapé

sofa

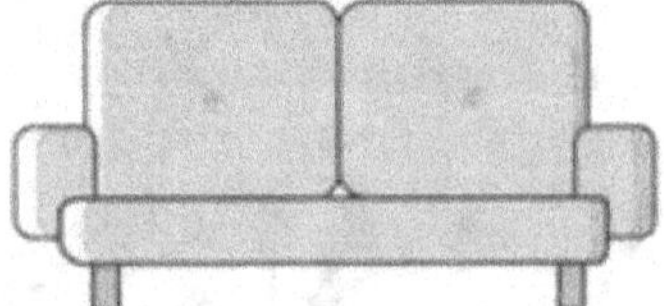

The sofa is comfortable to sit on.

coussins

poduszki

The cushion helps soften your seat.

téléphone

telefon

The telephone is ringing.

télévision

telewizja

That television is big.

haut-parleurs

głośniki

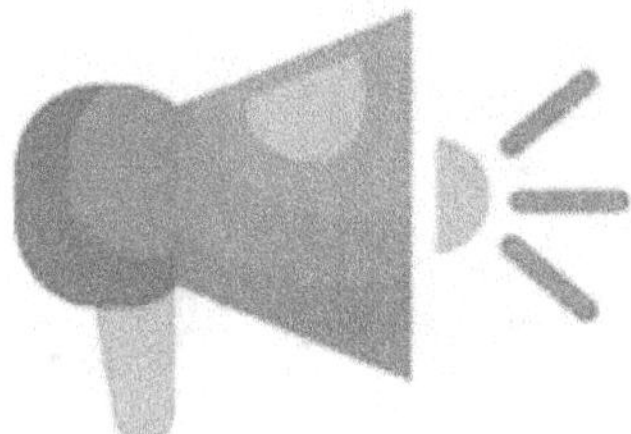

That speaker is used to increase the volume.

table d'appoint

stolik

That end table is sparkling clean.

service à thé

zestaw do herbaty

That tea set is from China.

cheminée

kominek

The fireplace makes me warm.

télécommandes

piloty

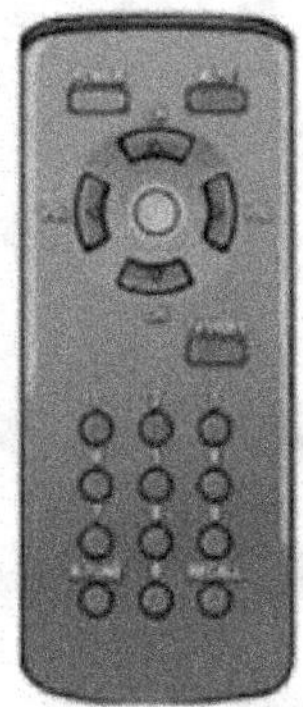

The remote has lots of buttons.

ventilateur électrique

wiatrak elektryczny

The fan is blowing wind.

lampadaire

lampa podłogowa

The floor lamp is very tall.

tapis

wykładzina podłogowa

The carpet is soft and silky.

bureaux

biurka

The table is made of wood.

stores

żaluzje

I will pull the blinds down.

rideaux

zasłony

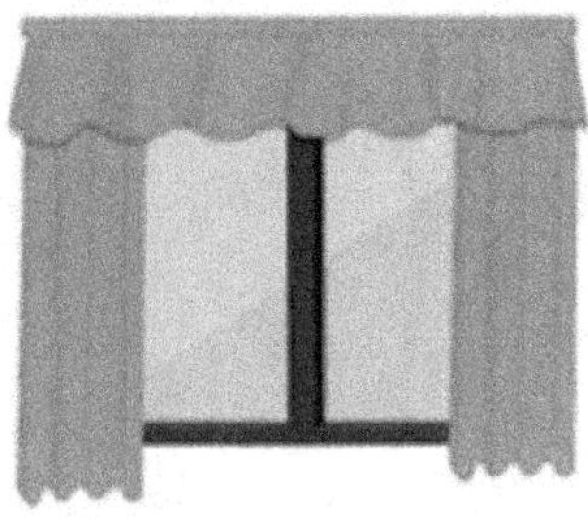

She opened the curtains.

image

obrazek

The picture is about the mountains and the sky.

vase

wazon

The roses are all in a vase.

l'horloge

zegar

The alarm clock is beeping.

oreiller

poduszka

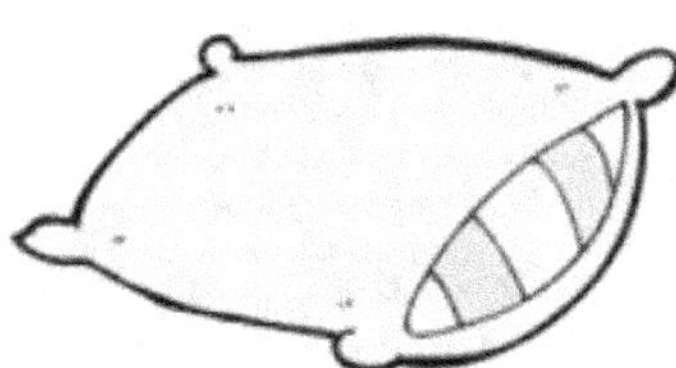

The pillow is pink and yellow.

cintre

wieszak na kapelusz

The hat stand has only one hat on it.

mettre la table

toaletka

I have made up on my dressing table.

lampe de table

lampa stołowa

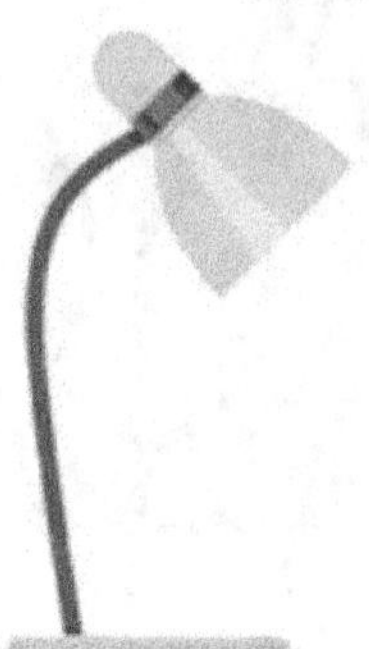

The table lamp will help me see in the dark.

miroir

lustro

The mirror is very tall.

planche a repasser

deska do prasowania

Don't touch the ironing board, it's hot!

boîte avec tiroir

pudełko z szufladą

You can keep your clothes in the hope chest.

table de chevet

stolik nocny

The nightstand has my lamp on it.

lit

łóżko

The bed is charming.

climatisation

klimatyzator

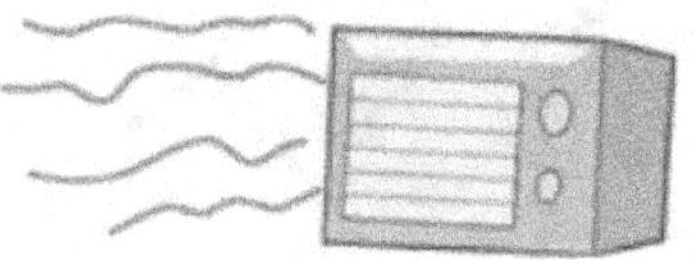

The air conditioner is cold.

cruche

dzbanek

The measuring jug has nothing inside.

dentifrice

pasta do zębów

The toothpaste is mint flavored.

brosse à dents

szczoteczka do zębów

The toothbrush has toothpaste on it.

savon

mydło

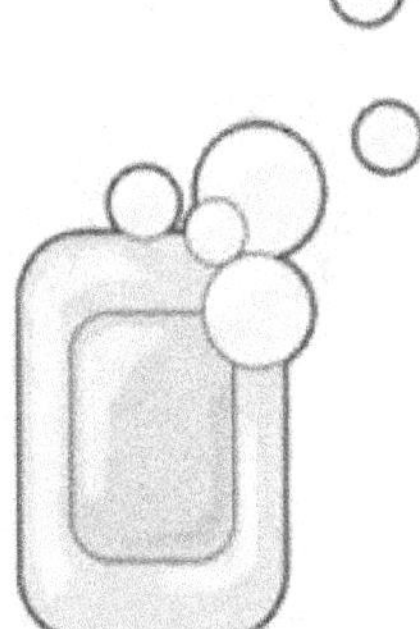

The soap is very bubbly.

pince à linge

clothespin

The clothespin will clip my clothes.

cintre

wieszak

The hanger is hanging my boots.

sèche-cheveux

suszarka do włosów

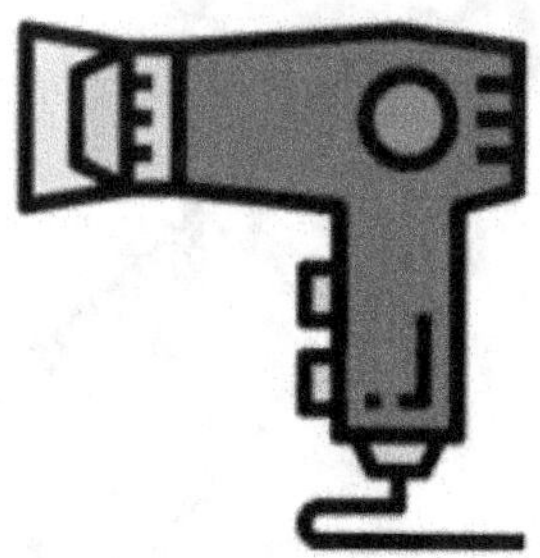

The hairdryer will blow my hair.

shampooing

szampon

The shampoo is used to clean your hair.

bulle

bańka

The bubbles are very fun to play in.

brosse

szczotka

She is brushing her hair with the brush.

papier toilette

papier toaletowy

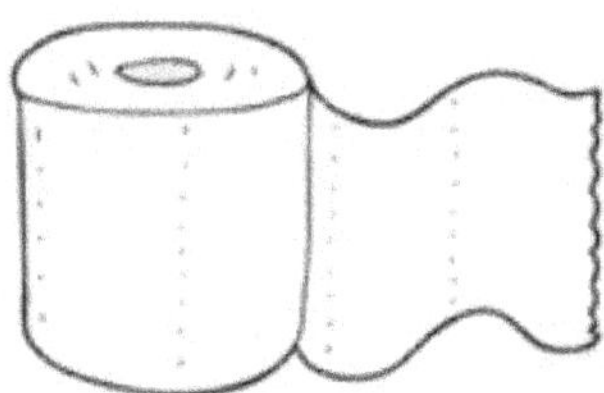

The toilet paper is used to dry your hands.

serviette

ręcznik

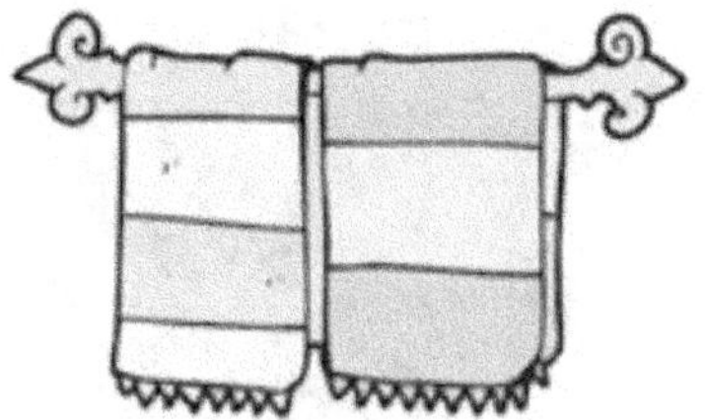

We have two towels on the rack.

corde à linge

sznur na bieliznę

My shirt is hanging on the clothesline.

douche

prysznic

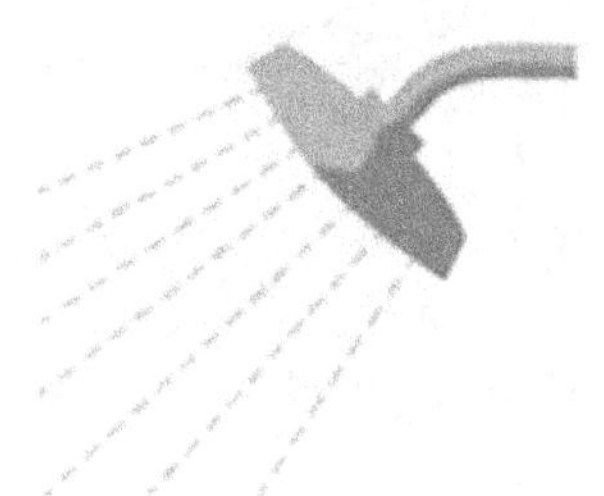

The shower is spraying water.

baignoire

wanna

The bathtub is comfortable.

lessive

proszek do prania

The laundry detergent is used with the washing machine.

seau

wiadro

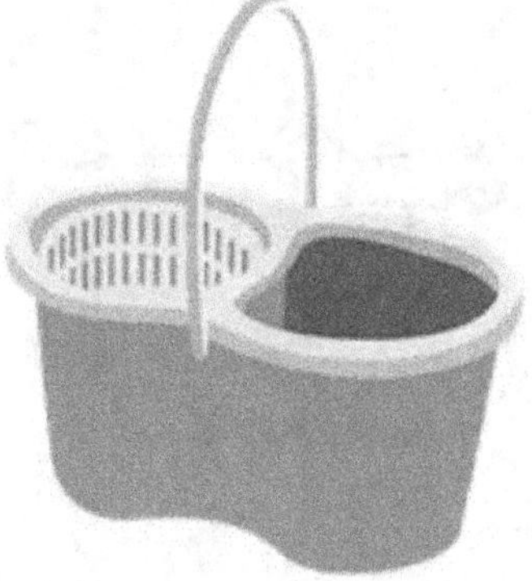

Can you help me fill up the bucket?

vadrouilles

mopy

The mop is used for mopping the floor.

savon liquide

mydło w płynie

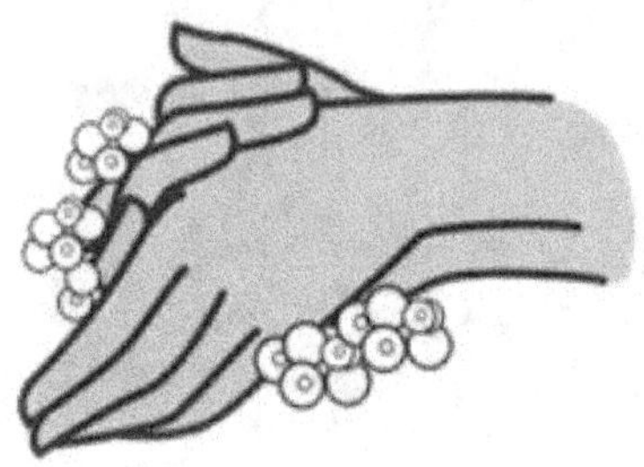

I use soapy water to wash my hands.

lessive en poudre

proszek do prania

I will scoop up the washing powder.

sac poubelle

worek na śmieci

The trash bag is full of trash.

poubelle

kosz na śmieci

You have only to put recylcle trash in the trash can.

les puits

umywalki

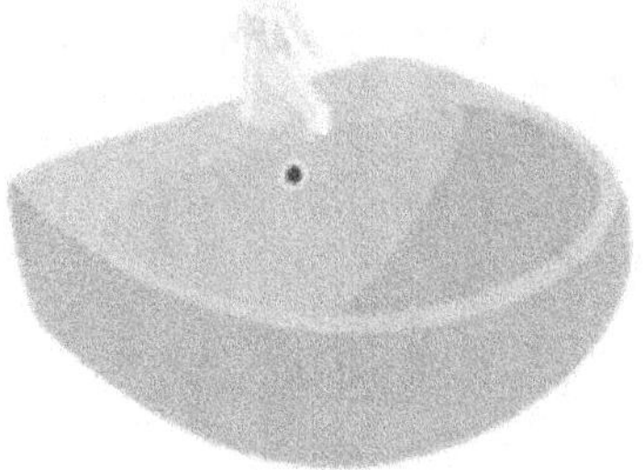

You should wash your hands in the sink.

cuvette des toilettes

muszla klozetowa

She let her bunny use the toilet.

machine à laver

pralka

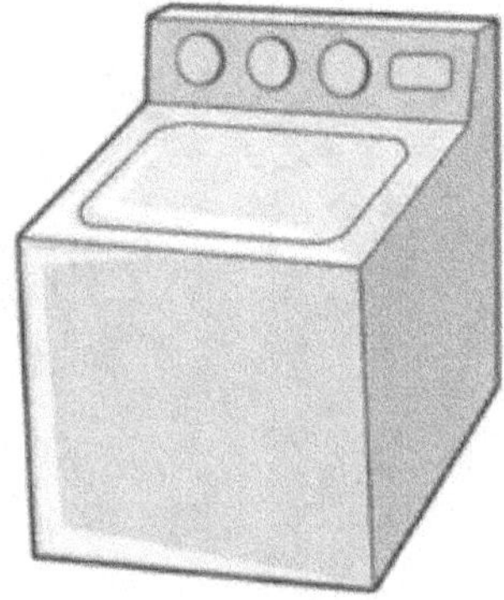

The washing machine wash your clothes.

panier à linge

kosz na pranie

She is putting all the clothes into the laundry basket.

le rasoir

brzytwa

He uses the razor to shave his beard.

rasoir électrique

maszynka elektryczna

The electric razor works faster than the normal one.

crème à raser

krem do golenia

The shaving cream is fluffy.

bain de bouche

płyn do płukania jamy ustnej

The mouthwash smells very lovely.

coton-tige

wacik

Q-tip can be used for many things.

brosse à cheveux

szczotka do włosów

She brushes her hair with her hairbrush.

peigne

grzebień

Her dad will comb her hair for her.

nettoyant

cleanser

Put the cap back on the cleanser bottle.

échelle

skala

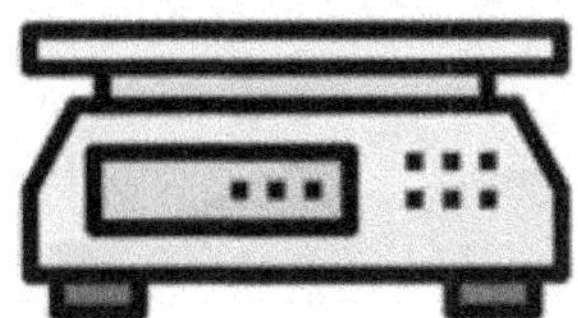

You can measure things on the scale.

papier de soie

papier bibułkowy

The tissue is on the counter.

jouets de bain

zabawki do kąpieli

The little duck is a bath toy.

robinet

kran

The faucet is broken.

miroir

lustro

He is looking in the mirror.

tapis de bain

dywanik łazienkowy

The bath mat is purple and yellow.

www.ingramcontent.com/pod-product-compliance
Lightning Source LLC
Chambersburg PA
CBHW082114170726
47999CB00015BA/2975